THE GREATEST GIFT

THE GREATEST GIFT

Reflections on International and Domestic Adoption

BETSY BUCKLEY

CREATIVE ARTS BOOK COMPANY
Berkeley California

The Greatest Gift is published by Donald S. Ellis
and printed by Creative Arts Book Company.

For information contact:
Creative Arts Book Company
833 Bancroft Way
Berkeley, California 94710
(800) 848-7789

ISBN 088739-339-X
Library of Congress Catalog Number 00-102319

Printed in Canada

Author's Note

In most cases, the names of individuals have been changed to protect their privacy. In a few other instances, specific details have been slightly altered for the same reason. In no way was the author's experience with the adoption process meant to represent the experience of every adopting family.

DEDICATION

For the biological parents of our children,
who gave the greatest gift;

for our children, Michael and Christie—
you are by far, the brightest stars
that light up our lives;

and for my parents, Dorothy and Kermit,
who taught me by example
to never give up.

TABLE OF CONTENTS

ACKNOWLEDGMENTS

A BOOK LIKE THIS IS A GROUP EFFORT THAT DRAWS UPON THE FEELINGS AND viewpoints of many contributors. To all who made the leap of faith to trust a stranger by sharing their stories, opinions, sorrows, joys and expertise, I am forever grateful. Thanks for risking to reveal your lives and the lives of your families. Though I have altered your names in an effort to protect your privacy, please know that it does not in any way diminish your contributions.

To Lauren Ludmerer, who helped ignite a spark within me, thanks. To Sharon Wahl and Lacy Schutz, whose knowledge helped tremendously in shaping this book, and to our social worker, Michael Carpenter, who shared his enthusiasm for my idea, and then shared valuable related resources, huge thanks. To my husband, who never said it couldn't be done, while at the same time enduring one too many bowls of cold cereal for dinner as his wife worked feverishly at the keyboard. Thanks to Craig and Carole Hostetler, Doug and Gail Wood, and Mary and Bill Fellenz, who allowed their children to be photographed for the book's cover, also to Robert George, for shooting a wonderful image. To Paige Smith for supplying me with some valuable statistics. To Mary Ebejer Petertyl for contributing to the international travel tips that appear in the appendix. To Marian McAndrews, the director of A.M.O.R. Adoptions, and to all the other agency representatives and experts for their unique contributions. To Sid Hollister, whose editorial expertise improved the piece. To my publisher, Donald Ellis, and the rest of his staff, thanks. A huge weight was lifted from my shoulders when you expressed an interest in publishing the manuscript. Finally, a heartfelt thanks to our son's biological parents for having the courage to ask for a better life for their son, and in so doing, enabled me to construct a book written out of love. This has been a journey like no other.

If by reading this book one person's fears are erased or his or her direction is clarified, my goal will have been accomplished. If I have dispelled one adoption myth, buried one prejudice, or smoothed the road for one more child to be adopted by a family that may not have previously considered adoption, my heart will be fuller.

Maybe, like Ernie's song from *Sesame Street* about wanting to visit the moon, the essence of life is not about what we wish for, but about finding out along the way that wishes do come true.

INTRODUCTION

THE IDEA OF WRITING A BOOK ON ADOPTION BEGAN TO TAKE SHAPE IN MY mind shortly after my husband brought our son home from Guatemala in October of 1995, although I had no idea how to go about it. I found myself becoming more and more interested in what other adopting parents had gone through. If there were other adoptive parents like me, people looking to share their experiences about adopting, then perhaps a book could come out of it.

I knew the journal I'd kept throughout the adoption process was valuable and useful, and I had many thoughts and feelings I wanted to convey about infertility and the journey into adoption. I also had a computer and the encouragement and support of friends and relatives. What I needed, though, was a larger scope of experiences, including those of other individuals who were embarking upon the same path. Did other infertile women dread going to baby showers as I had? Did other adoptive parents at one time or another during the process feel isolated and unsure? Had other parents lost an assignment? What was it like for other people raising adopted children? Was it any different for them than raising a biological child? How did other parents tell their children they were adopted? What were other adoptive parents' fears? I hoped I would learn some answers.

Initially, I was unsure how to go about getting answers to these questions while caring for my new son. Then, I worried if I would I get any responses at all? Would people share their intimate experiences with me, a complete stranger? I was primarily interested in people's feelings, not simply a recitation of chronological facts. I began to solicit participants with a twenty-five-item questionnaire on infertility, parenting, and adoption that I mailed—or handed out—to support groups and agencies around the country. Enlisting the help of these groups, I then asked them to pass the questionnaire on to willing adoptive parents and to those considering adoption.

Here's a sampling of some of the questions: Why did you want to have children? Was your first desire to have a biological child? What family traditions are you planning to pass along to your children? What were your feelings/your spouse's feelings when you first considered adoption? Did those feelings change over time? Were friends and family supportive of your decision to adopt? How important is it/was it to adopt a child of your ethnicity? What was your biggest fear during the adoption process? Any regrets? Participants were asked to write down responses only to those questions they felt comfortable with.

In addition to the questionnaire, I explored the Internet—a growing presence in more and more lives. There was, however, one small problem: how did I go about using it? At the time, I had no idea. So, in addition to bathing, feeding, playing with, caring for and bonding with our new son (while probably neglecting my husband), I was teaching myself how to send an e-mail message, selecting and subscribing to an on-line service, hunting for related user groups, and attempting to try and understand the Worldwide Web.

What I discovered was that cyberspace is a great way to access information for an endless number of topics, including all the issues that were of interest to me. It's possible, as demonstrated by one woman's story, to locate children that are available for adoption by using the internet. Also, more and more agencies are preparing web sites to spread the word about their organizations, their policies and their goals. So are many attorneys who handle private adoption cases. Many other resources, like the National Federation of Open Adoption Education, have a web site with an e-mail address. It's even possible to view on screen the faces of children needing caring homes! Connecting via the Internet and the Worldwide Web with others who have already "made the trip," or with professionals in the field, gave me rapid access to a wealth of information—information that the majority of prospective adoptive parents need and want. At times, the processes of both domestic and international adoptions can make people feel like they're in a tiny boat crossing a huge sea, and no land is in sight.

I might add a word of advice to those who have yet to become familiar with this electronic mail system. Sharing information this way is often a gigantic leap of faith. The information exchanged is only as reliable and honest as the people involved. Most of the people offering opinions, asking questions or merely learning, have never met, and probably never will.

When introducing my project and myself on the Internet, I proceeded very gently. Browsing the Network, I was able to locate individuals who were subscribing to adoption, infertility, international and parenting user-groups. The next step was simply to ask: would you be willing to share your feelings and experiences? During the course of a year's time, the answer became a resounding yes! That in itself is a telling fact. Adoptive parents, professionals and professional organizations involved with adoption do, and did, have a lot to say about this life-altering event. Many parents told me that they responded in order to help others with their decisions, hoping to make someone else's journey a little less stressful and a little more assured than theirs had been. Other parents told me they simply felt good recounting their experiences. Whatever their motivation, some people had to relive terrible heartbreaks, while others could once again enjoy their triumphs.

As it turned out, using the Internet became my primary medium for collecting stories and information. It was clearly the fastest way to hear from people of many ethnic and religious groups, all at once. In the end, the responses came from every section of the country, in total representing twenty-seven different states. (Some participants asked to remain anonymous, so locating them was not possible.) I corresponded with one family living in Canada, and an agency director who was living and working in Russia. By far, the greatest number of participants were living in the state of Texas. The youngest parent at the time of a first adoption was twenty-three, and the oldest, by the husband's own admission "a mite older than I should have been," was fifty-two. I heard from parents who were denied adoption, from those who have adopted only one child, and from parents who adopted several. Of those I contacted, a woman with nine internationally adopted children holds the record for having the largest adoptive family. Other people who were both biological and adoptive parents, or foster parents first, also shared their stories. Finally, I personally interviewed several individuals who were living in the Midwest, including one woman who shared her innermost thoughts about adopting a four-year-old boy who was born in Russia.

In the end, I learned many things, primarily because people came to trust me. I was accepted as another adoptive parent. Since I was in most instances a faceless, voiceless entity, I tried to be as compassionate and empathetic as possible. I learned about Korea's Thanksgiving Day, known as Ch'Usok, celebrated on the fifteenth day of the eighth lunar month, when Koreans offer thanks to their ancestors for a good harvest. I learned that military families often have a difficult time adopting because of their lack of a permanent residence. I learned that ideas vary as to how much American culture should be integrated into the life of an internationally adopted child, and about the importance many countries place on the presence of religion in the lives of adoptive parents. I learned about the difficulties single parents face when adopting, and about orphanages in China. I also learned how dreaded the word, "hero," had become to an overwhelming number of adoptive parents, and how frequently it popped up in their conversations.

Finally, I learned much about the human spirit—about fortitude, strength, resourcefulness, perseverance and hope. I learned, also, to what degree people were willing to open up their souls to a stranger, revealing the wide range of circumstances that characterizes domestic and international adoption. Along the way I made a few friends.

THE GREATEST GIFT

CHAPTER 1

First Comes Love, Then Comes Marriage...

LIKE MANY WOMEN BORN INTO THE BABY BOOMER GENERATION OF THE 1950s, I was raised in the shadows of the traditional family unit. Mom stayed home for part of my childhood, and Dad went off to work. Ours was a happy, middle-class suburban life. My mother miscarried two times between my brother's birth and my own, so when I arrived, my parents were thrilled. It was implied throughout my childhood that falling in love, getting married, and having a family were the quintessential elements to a meaningful life. And I thought, naively, that it would be easy to achieve—Ozzie and Harriet made it look easy to achieve, and so did June and Ward Cleaver.

I had rehearsed many times over my life's plan for the period between the ages of eighteen and thirty, and the plot never varied: meet my knight in shining armor, fall in love, have a lovely outdoor wedding under big billowy white tents, give birth to beautiful children, then live life to its fullest. My due dates would land in the springtime, a perfect season in the Midwest, a time when the redbuds and dogwoods bloom and the air is sweetly scented. As a couple, I imagined we would be in complete control of our future and not let pregnancy happen to us like a shock wave or a random shooting star. We'd responsibly plan the number of children we'd have by considering the overpopulation of the world. We'd limit ourselves to two and no more. The road that lay before me then seemed unending.

1

HIGH ANXIETY AND THE EMOTIONAL MELTDOWN

Looking back, my twenties breezed by like a record skipping over three or four songs. Suddenly, it seemed, I was approaching the thirty-mile marker and was still entrenched in furthering my career with no man or child in sight. I began passing off my single situation in conversations with, "Oh, I'm a late bloomer." Then, somewhere between thirty-one and thirty-three it happened: I began to feel the squeeze of not having what I wanted: a caring husband and loving children.

Almost overnight, the sight of another mother pushing a child on a park swing set me into a crying jag that lasted for hours. In meetings, rather than being attentive to my duties as an art director, my concentration was fixed out the window on the cherub-faced eight-and ten-month-olds who were regularly strolled on the corporate grounds by their daycare providers. Rather than being lost in brainstorming a great idea for a new cereal or dog food, I was drifting in a daydream much as I had done in eighth-grade French class when the lessons started getting difficult. "Where had all the time gone?" This thought was repetitiously and unmercifully playing over and over and over in my mind like the rat-a-tat-tat of a woodpecker. A cute child with her happy parents playing over there meant a little stab in the heart here.

From all outward appearances my life was well adjusted, but inside I was a whirling tornado like the *Looney Tunes* character, the "Tasmanian Devil." I felt like all of the three faces of Eve. I could swing through a wide range of emotions quicker than some women could put on their make up. Something had taken control of my feelings, something alien. And then there was *The Waltons*—I wished some television executive would please take those wholesome family-centered reruns off the air before I drowned in self-pity! By the time the end of the show neared and all the Walton kids routinely whispered "Good night," I was a sniffling idiot who could barely see the screen through her puffy, reddened eyes.

Conversely, some days I woke up feeling like I could bite the head off a doll.

This drawn out time-bomb phenomenon was worse, it seemed, than the one big shock of having a heart attack. This was slow, slow torture, as bad as water dripping on your forehead, one lousy drop at a time.

Everywhere I looked I saw (or imagined I saw) joyous families: Mom, Dad, little Suzie, brother Bobby and the dog. They were running in the park, chasing after a Frisbee, cruising down the supermarket aisles, in front of me at the theater, in the rear-view mirror behind me at the drive-through window, at the art museum standing behind the marbled nudes, peeking over opened books at the public library.

When would I start my family? "Why is there no one for *me?*" I asked out loud, as if someone besides the dog would hear me and send an answer down from heaven. Like pouring salt into an already open wound, my acquaintances were saying, "You're attractive. I can't believe you're not married yet." I wanted to snarl.

To make matters worse, I had accomplished much of what I'd wanted to accomplish in other areas of my life. I'd worked with some talented and funny creative professionals in my field of advertising. I'd traveled to many of the cities I'd wanted to see, vacationed where and when I wanted, and had accumulated enough possessions to meet the needs of my modest lifestyle. Even that sleek pair of suede slacks I'd had my eyes on for the longest time were now hanging in my closet, and that decadently expensive perfume I'd appreciated in Neiman Marcus was adorning my body. I had a devoted passion for horseback riding and enough engaging friends to suit me. But I shared all this with no one special person. I wanted to fall in love and be loved. Why was this so difficult to accomplish?

This basic human desire, along with my need to procreate, turned into a compulsion. It was changing and challenging every aspect of my life. Even my once-rewarding career was losing its appeal—fast. "There must be something more to life," I began crying, as I dragged my sleepy body through the motions of getting dressed in order to be "alertly" seated in my office by what I considered the offensive hour of 8 A.M. "All this rushing—for what?" I was emotionally and physically drained. I felt as if I had just done ten rounds with George Foreman, but without the bruise marks to prove it. I wasn't able to concentrate on anything other than falling in love and having a baby. At day's end, I raced home to hide in silence alone on the sofa. All the lessons I'd learned about positive thinking were gone. "Why me?" When I looked in the mirror, I blamed my encroaching wrinkles and untoned abdomen for my sorry situation.

By the time my thirty-fourth birthday rolled around, and after several short-lived romantic relationships, I was turning into someone I didn't want to know. I found myself out of control and out of orbit: I was a desperate woman. All I thought about was having a baby, or, rather, not having a baby. In this bleak period, I would have done practically anything to know what it was like to have an unusual food craving—pickles...ice cream...chocolate syrup...pickles on top of ice cream with chocolate syrup. I obsessed. I cursed.

Somewhere in the middle of this personal chaos, my last redeeming characteristic was faltering: my usual determined, healthy self-esteem. I was my own worst critic. Maybe my standards for a soul mate were too high? Maybe I should lower them? Doubt crept in slowly, then took hold like a vengeful flu and wouldn't let go. During these months of anguish, I never intentionally broke something in anger, though it probably would have done me some good. What I did do was imagine what a wild horse must have felt like when it was first roped and ridden. In the end, I felt defeated, transformed into something unnatural. Then I realized I needed professional help. This had turned into something bigger than I could handle alone.

PROFESSIONAL HELP TO THE RESCUE

In her office, the therapist pushed the box of tissues closer to me. After some introductory chitchat we dug in to the heart of the matter.

"What's brought you here?" she asked. Her pen was poised to strike, a look of compassion on her face. With her seventy-five-dollar-an-hour fee whirling around in my mind, I responded immediately.

"A baby. I want to have a baby, and I feel like I'm running out of time." I recall blurting it out so quickly that I surprised even myself. It sounded so harsh.

"Oh, I see," she said. Her voice trailed off at the end of the sentence, carrying with it a dreadful pitying tone. She lowered her eyes. Her simple, yet telling reply seemed to speak of many long, difficult sessions to come. She sounded doubtful. I found myself wondering if this was her usual reaction, the result of hearing the same story one too many times. I sensed that it would have made her happier if I'd spoken of infidelity, or unresolved sibling rivalry. Would she be able to understand my feelings of hopelessness and fear? I felt more alone and more angry. Would she be able to understand the numbing haze in which I was living? What about my feelings of emptiness and anxiety? Her desk picture showed beaming faces of a smiling man, presumably her husband, and a contented child. I could only hope. I wanted her to be my fairy god-mother and wave her wand in the air to change everything overnight.

"I feel like a walking billboard when I go out on dates," I told her—ATTRACTIVE, SINGLE WOMAN WITH AGING SKIN AND DWINDLING HORMONES SEEKS TO MARRY ATTRACTIVE, SUC-CESSFUL, KIND MAN WITH WHOM TO HAVE A FAMILY WHILE I STILL HAVE TIME!

"I suppose I was looking at men as prospective fathers first, and husbands, second. I was running them off before we sat down to din-ner. 'I'll have a steak,' he'd say. 'I'll have a baby,' I'd say." (In hindsight, on those occasions when I was not so blatantly offensive, I was uncon-sciously undermining my efforts by asking intimate personal details too soon. I fast-forwarded half a dozen dates this way, and wondered at the time why no one phoned back.)

She looked stunned.

By now I could tell this "problem" was going to cost me a lot of money. The therapist had turned her note pad over to its second page and was busily making more notes. I continued to reveal my story over the course of the next few weeks.

"At twenty-one, my newly married friends were all having babies," I said. My days were spent attending one baby shower after another. Seemingly, just the day before we had been sunning ourselves, lustily eyeing the guys at the pool and talking about what we were going to do with the rest of the summer."

"Go on."

"My pregnant friends, understandably, grew distant. They spoke of handmade baby bonnets, washing bottles and nipples, deciding whether to breast feed or not, knowing how to distinguish a colicky cry from one of hunger, maintaining a good sex life after the baby arrived and everything else connected with parenthood. It was like eavesdrop-ping on a group of people speaking Swahili. Part of me wanted to know motherhood as they were beginning to, and another part of me thought that they were becoming parents before they had the opportunity to do other things with their lives."

She put down her pen and leaned back fully in the chair. On subsequent visits to her office I confided, "I've even been to a psychic." Desperate people do desperate things. I hesitated for a moment after that revelation, searching her face for some type of horrified reaction, though I never got it. "I went for the sole purpose of having her tell me if I would marry and when it would be. And children. I asked her about having children."

By now, I figured, the therapist thought I'd gone mad.

DO THE CARDS HOLD THE ANSWERS?

Rita, the Greek mystic with a thick accent who held my hands to read my palms, said I was promised two children in this lifetime: a boy and a girl. She cautioned, "But not for three more years." Her jet black hair was piled high on the top of her head like the beauticians who used to style my mother's hair (and in-between the rinse and set, offer me a Coke). Consequently, Rita looked familiar, and her eyes were honest.

As the words, "a boy and a girl," came tumbling from her lips, my thoughts went back to a game I had played with my friends as a young adult. The game foretold a person's fate. Like an off-limits game of OUIJA played inside a closet hidden from the view of parents, this game was greatly anticipated. More than once, a few girlfriends and I gathered in the living room of my parents' home to see what the future had in store for us. Huddled together like football players around a quarterback, we picked the steadiest of the group to dangle a sewing needle carefully from a long thread over a chosen girl's pulsing wrist. That was supposedly the spot where a person's energy was channeled. Miraculously, the needle would begin moving on its own power. If the needle swung two times, then that person was going to have two children, if it swung six times before stopping, then that person was going to have six children, and so on. And the way the needle swung was very important in determining gender: if it swung in a circle, then that girl would give birth to a boy; if it swung in a diagonal line, a girl. After the first "response," the dangler would dip the needle alongside the person's wrist three times to "clear it," then do it all over again. Whenever the needle moved more than three times, a pained expression swept over the face of the girl in question. When we played this game with expectant friends, somehow, it proved to be accurate, at least in predicting gender. As for me? A boy and a girl, in that order. Maybe Rita would be right?

After digressing into that distant past, I screamed, "Three more years! But I don't want to wait that long!"

She looked up from my hands and into my eyes. "Betsy, everything happens for a reason. Think of it as a learning experience."

A learning experience? I was beginning to think I had wasted my money.

"Don't worry. It will be all right. Right now, men are sensing that you're in a hurry. The next major change I see will occur around your thirty-fourth birthday."

I remember letting out an audible groan.

"Ask for divine guidance and put the matter out into the universe. Write down the qualities that you are looking for in a man, and ask for all the negativity to leave. Right now, you see some qualities you admire in this man, some in that man, and some in another."

It sounded to me like she could have been describing a refrigerator rather than a man— "This one cools better, this one is larger, this one is longer lasting."

After she shuffled the thick tarot cards, I was asked to cut them into three uneven stacks. As she turned the cards over, one after another, I calculated in my head— "if she means marriage at thirty-four, that'll give me six more years to have my two-child family." My mother's premature death at fifty-four fueled my desire to have a family by forty. I knew it was becoming more culturally acceptable for women to wait until forty or later to have their first babies; science was making it safer and careers often dictated it. But I didn't want to leave my children at the same tender age I was left if something, God forbid, happened to me. I wanted youthfulness and vigor on my side.

She went on. "I see the number four. You will meet the man you are destined to marry in either four days, four weeks, or four months. He will approach you from behind, and I see you sitting outside at a table."

Destiny. That idea was so fluid, so nebulous, that my own hard reality of twenty-four hour torment couldn't get hold of it, much less fully examine it. Was it possible that my life had a determined path and mine was to be childless? Had Marco Polo been destined to explore much of the Asian continent? What about George Washington? Was he destined to become our first president from the time he was a little boy? What about Abraham Lincoln? Was he destined to die as revealed in his dream? Was my fate really revealed in my hands, in the stars, up in the heavens, or in the hands of God? Had my fate already been dictated by the precise moment of my birth, governed by the alignment of the constellations? Could a person change her destiny? I left the psychic that day feeling even more unsure of my future than when I had first sat down.

On subsequent visits, she said that I was bringing fears into this life from a past life.

"You mean I've had another life?" I asked incredulously. That was a thought I hadn't entertained before.

"Yes," she said. She paused, looked down at the cards, scooted her sliding glasses back onto her nose and said, "In your last life you died in childbirth. The child lived...but you did not...though you will eventually rise above."

"Rise above what?" I asked myself all the way home.

Approximately four months later I met Charlie.

OLD WESTERNS, HOP SCOTCH AND THE BOOGEY MONSTER

It was during therapy that I examined the reasons for wanting a family in the first place. It certainly wasn't because the birthing process seemed so appealing. In fact, for some time after attending so many baby showers where women talked of five-inch long C-section scars, swollen ankles, lifelong stretch marks, back pain, breaking water, stubborn weight gain and tender hemorrhoids, you couldn't have paid me enough money to go through with it, drugs or no drugs. The umbilical cord sounded like something from a space odyssey. Childbirth as depicted in Western movies certainly was less than an idyllic, blissful experience. The women always howled long and loudly. My stomach still gets queasy whenever I remember the scenes of someone running off to get wet rags or to boil water. I recalled thinking how lucky I was to live in this century, when holistic birthing rooms with soft, gentle lighting had replaced the rough, log-cabin living of the pioneers.

Rooted somewhere in my psyche there was a real fear of the entire process. What if something went wrong? I asked myself, "How could women not think about that possibility while carrying?" My wild, rambling mind, I was sure, would conjure up the worst. By the time nine months rolled around, I would probably expect to give birth to an alien form.

In fact, though, rather than accept the negative ideas as gospel, I sifted through the influential elements and settled upon my own set of reasons for wanting a child. It was a consideration like most others— it had its pros and cons.

One reason was the element of surprise. The physical blending of two distinctly different people in the production of a third is one of the greatest and most uncontrollable surprises left in an adult's life: I think it's going to be a boy...no, it's a girl!... look at her hair!... she's got her uncle Al's curly red hair... look at her nose! ...where did she get that mole?... maybe from your mother's side of the family...I wonder if she'll be tall when she grows up, like the rest of us FitzSimmons? That same sort of gleeful surprise holds true for the development of personality. The opportunity to witness the nuances of character as they develop and unfold before your eyes, growing and changing, is nothing less than remarkable. Children are a surprising combination of spontaneous and cultivated learning, often with varied results: "William's such a quiet child, Taylor is so much more demanding than her brother, and Alex, he isn't like either of us. I just don't understand it." The biggest, perhaps most magical surprise of all, is looking into the innocent eyes of a newborn, and asking, "What do you suppose she'll be when she grows up?"

Having a family also creates companionship, another reason for wanting children. Splashing in a puddle together, watching your child inspect a firefly and turn it, against your better judgment, into a glowing "ring;" washing the muted, chalky pinks and blues from the driveway after hopscotch is over, or building a tree house together. It's about whirling the jump rope as your kids jump, jump, jump, about losing a kite in a tree and climbing up dangerously too high to retrieve it. It's catching butterflies with your son and watching your daughter appear as a giant lady bug in the school play or putting together a tea-party with both of you dressed up in heels and frilly skirts. It's about helping make a "house" from opened umbrellas, and waiting for your moment to appear as the tooth fairy.

With a child in your company, you can indulge in childish pleasures, stripping away the layers of defenses built up over years of adult living. Running under a sprinkler, going barefoot, making papier mache masks, finger-painting, dying Easter eggs, climbing a tree, hiding under the covers from the boogey monster can liberate the stodgiest adult.

Porcelain Dolls with Real Hair, Passed from Mother to Child, Generation After Generation

A third reason for wanting children was for tradition. I wanted to pass along the special moments from my childhood—much as my parents had done with me, and their parents with them—and in the process, become more aware myself of the values, moral structure and idiosyncrasies that made my family—like every family—unique. Tradition grants a person the chance to appreciate the cycles of life, birth, growth and death. Family traditions bridge gaps and fill in some of the empty spaces that creep into a person's life. Carrying out meaningful traditions, whether it be eating smoked goose for dinner every Christmas instead of turkey, or building a race car for Soap Box Derby Day in the same methodical way your father did, regardless of the poor results, builds a foundation from which character can grow.

One of my favorite rituals from childhood was making chocolate fudge every Saturday night. My father would hover around the simmering pot like a hen carefully tending its eggs, tenderly nurturing the bubbling goo. The squat glass filled with water on top of the stove told the candy's fate as my father periodically tested his mixture, dripping a little of it from a long-handled wooden spoon into the water. Too long on the stove, the fudge would be hard as concrete; not cooked long enough, a sticky unmanageable mess.

In its best sense, tradition is a harmonious gift, and it carries with it the chance to teach. Teaching fishing by baiting a hook, casting out, reeling in, then sending the wet, floppy thing back to where it came from; teaching how to ride a bike without a push from behind; or how to make a dam from rocks and mud; teaching the skills to negotiate obstacles like the school bully, thereby sparing your child a blackened eye; teaching right from wrong and when to say, "No," instead of "Not now." It's the opportunity to help another person become the best he or she can be.

FOR IMMORTALITY

Another reason for wanting children surfaced while I paged through our family's photo albums, a collection of memorabilia that had been stored in crooked stacks in the hall closet. Two albums were intact, neatly and completely, filled with tiny pictures with scalloped edges. Other albums were missing a picture or two on every page like the front teeth absent from a youngster's smile. Other albums were crammed with too many photos, photos with dog-eared corners and creases down their middles, which left the faces of relatives eerily split in half.

In these albums were images that told stories. Stories of my father as a young boy proudly facing the camera, his arm wrapped around the neck of his beloved dog, Rusty. I wondered if even as a young boy he dreamed of becoming a father one day. Stories of my mother and father as a married couple dressed up in Halloween costumes as Greta Garbo and Humphrey Bogart; barefooted after wading in the river at a friend's summer house; bent over their mallets while playing croquet; standing by the Christmas tree in "fancy clothes." This visual condensation of a life, a marriage, and then a family was overwhelming. After paging through the last album, I realized that I didn't want to be a stop sign in the middle of the road, or a sawed-off branch in our family tree. And most assuredly, I didn't want some relative looking at my photo thirty years into the future as I stood alone and solemn-faced on the pages of another dog-eared photo album.

CHAPTER 2

It's Off to the Races

WHEN I WAS A YOUNG GIRL, MY MOTHER USED TO SING ME ONE PARTICULAR song over and over. In it, she called me her sunshine. Indeed, I was her sunshine, and she, mine. This was also the tune that played almost three decades later when I pulled on the string from a stuffed elephant that hung on display in the department store. Music can stop the world. It stopped mine that day, for an instant, taking me back twenty-five years, to days of consoling kisses, homemade cookies and lemonade stands. Favorite songs link us to moments in time, evoking memories, for better or worse, of our proms, picnics, weddings, bar mitzvahs, barn dances and childhood. This song bridged the gap between generations. I longed to sing it to my own children someday.

Not being pregnant didn't stop me from surveying all the merchandise available for babies and moms: items new and sometimes frightening. Pillows to keep babies' heads in place while placed in car seats, tiny plastic tubs for bathing in the sink, teethers to be chilled in the refrigerator, diaper genies to swirl away the smell of soiled diapers. Then there were the bottles: tall bottles, short bottles, glass ones or plastic; bottles needing plastic liners and bottles with hard tops; straight bottles and bottles bent for easier feeding: undecorated bottles and bottles imprinted with balls and kittens. And there were nipples: some with stubby squared-off tips, some with longer tips bulging at the ends; clear nipples and dark brown nipples; nipples for the large as well as the small-mouthed baby, and everything else in between. Of course there were also diapers: plastic, plain white cloth and disposable. Some even had happy faces that disappeared when the inevitable had happened.

It was night after night of the same old thing. Go to work. Come home. Feed the dogs. Turn on the television. Fix dinner. Go to bed. Get up. Go to work. Come home. Read a book. Take a bath. Feed the dogs. Skip dinner. Go to bed.

I'd studied the possible suitors within my work environment for the last two years. Though one prospect caught my eye, he was too young, a not-yet-ready-for-a-baby kind of guy. No others popped to the surface. Within a few nights of this sad realization, I sat down by the fireplace, and wrote the following: Attractive, physically fit, professional who loves the outdoors, Bob Dylan, horses, wide open spaces, and unconventionality, looking for professional 30-40, with morals, for possible relationship.

This became the ad I placed in the personals section of the local newspaper; it underwent six or seven scribbled versions before I was satisfied. Yet it seemed worse than having to write one's own obituary.

Later, I thought, "with morals?" Just what did I mean by that? Who doesn't have morals?

Nevertheless, sixty-five men must have thought they had morals, for that's how many responses I solicited. An overwhelming number, I thought. At first glance, there appeared to be no quacks, no geeks, and no still-living-at-home-with-mother types, that so many of my friends had warned me of. I did feel a little odd, though, sorting through the masses of men. It was like separating the laundry into different piles. This was dating in the 90s? Some guys left phone messages, some sent pictures, some did both. In one photo, a guy wore a gold necklace so tightly that it looked as though it must have been choking him. Another was standing, shirtless, alongside his boat. (I liked the looks of the boat.) One guy professed to be a librarian; another, an engineer. One guy liked to tour Missouri wine country on his Harley. One guy was a pilot. One guy had a pot belly; another was balding. I trimmed the candidates down to seven. One of those, Charlie, mailed a picture of himself with his dog. It arrived in a scented pale blue envelope that he had splashed with aftershave. Now this was someone I could love.

I felt relieved. Here, at last, was a potential prospect. "Make sure you meet him somewhere safe," many of my girlfriends chirped in unison. And so, when I phoned him later to make arrangements for our first meeting, I had relied upon the standard formula for a blind date—meet over lunch—if he turned out to be a dud, I would be able to leave gracefully after just one hour.

We both described our wardrobes on the morning before our meeting. When I arrived, I began searching the entire restaurant, inside and out, for the same cute, inviting man who had a dog waiting for him at home. Then something disappointing happened. I never found my potential prospect! Appearing as though I had been stood up, I stomped back to my car. I felt red in the face. Once back at my office, I had calmed down a little bit.

"How did it go," asked my closest coworker with a sheepish look on her face.

"He didn't show," I said.

"He what?" she asked incredulously.

"He didn't show," I said louder, this time a with a little agitation in my voice.

"Oh, no."

"Oh, yes."

"Men."

"Yeah, men." I reiterated.

After a long pause, she eventually got around to saying, "Hey, I've got a neighbor who's kind of cute and nice."

"No thanks. I'm not interested. Besides, I still have six other guys to try in the keepers pile."

About seven days passed, when I received a phone call from my missed blind date. Later, he confessed, he was embarrassed about the entire mishap. He thought he saw me based upon my description, but was a little unsure. Besides, he added, by the time he determined that it must be me, I was stomping off to my car like Gunga Din ready to trounce the enemy.

Fortunately, there was something in his timidity that I found appealing, so we decided to arrange a second meeting at the same location. This time, we found each other. And this time I didn't need to use the end of my lunch hour as a reason to leave. I was enjoying myself.

He looked like the kind of man who would pick up an injured bird from the sidewalk and put it back into its nest. After we parted and my work day was over, I returned home and went to my sorted pile of personal ad responses. All remaining six prospects were dropped into the trash.

After our auspicious beginning, we continued to date and explore our personalities and wishes, as most couples do when attempting to form a new relationship. I did, indeed, learn that he was tender, and that he had been married before and enjoyed being step-dad to two, now grown, boys. With my family-driven ambition, that was a definite plus in his favor.

"It was one chance in a million," my dad said, that I should fall in love and marry someone I met through placing an ad. But I did. At the even riper-and-readier age of thirty-five, after almost two years of getting to know one another, I married Charlie in Wyoming among tall aspens and lodgepole pines. I had found my needle in the haystack, and a man as desiring of a family as I.

LET THE ADVICE BEGIN

We weren't even married when the flood of unsolicited questions and commentary came pouring in from all directions.

"Are you planning on a family?...When are you going to start?...How many children do you think you'll be having?...Two's a nice number. Isn't your husband too old for children?...At your ages, I wouldn't wait too long to start...Most men really do want a son to carry on their name."

Before we had even said our "I do's", I again felt hurried.

My new husband and I moved quickly to begin a family. We took our positions at the starting line—he, at forty-three, and I, thirty-five. We hastened the getting-to-know-each-other phase for the sake of time, disregarding the family planning advice that suggested we wait at least a year before attempting to start a family, a year that would give our marriage, or any marriage, solid footing. Like many couples surveyed, we felt that we were rapidly approaching the cutoff period for conception. After 40, a woman's chances of conception steadily declines. Here it was again, ticking time, forcing us to fast-forward our marriage. With the passing of every cycle, I was sure my eggs were losing their fertility. This was definitely a race.

My husband and I began our endeavor, like many couples, hopeful—hopeful that any day, any month, we would achieve a pregnancy. I was aware of my mother's two miscarriages, but knew of no other part of either of our pasts that seemed to hint at the fertility problems we were soon to experience.

I purchased a book on everything a person needed to know to get pregnant—just in case. "What Couples Need To Know Right Now," screamed the subtitle. Soon I was adding elements to or eliminating elements from our lifestyles like a spring cleaning—throwing out all that was of no use and replacing it with useful things. Not such an easy task at forty-three and thirty-five. Caffeine was out: drinking only one cup of coffee a day cut a person's chances of conceiving in half. Vitamins A, B1, B6, and D were in. Out were our chocolates, our sodas and our headache medicines. In was broccoli, pasta, turkey and yogurt. Out went processed foods and frozen dinners, forcing me to cook real foods. Out went the electric blanket (even this, apparently, contributed to the inability to conceive).[1] In its place, on a good day, came warm hugs.

We were familiar with the obvious conception blockers—alcohol, drugs, sexually transmitted diseases, and stress—but neither of us had any idea, until reading about it, that radiation waves from the backs of our computer monitors could be responsible for the inability to conceive. We both sat at them every day! One study reported that continued exposure to radiation can cause biological stress that interferes with the hormones responsible for reproduction.[2] Upon learning this, I immediately found proof, or thought I found proof, in a coworker. She and her husband were childless after eight tormenting years. I could see it in her eyes. She sat zombie-eyed behind her computer, day after day after day, completely miserable. Was this what was in store for me? A pitiful remnant of a vibrant woman?

Other potential hazards: lead, hair spray, nail polish solvents, pesticides, electrical office equipment, microwaves. Hazards were everywhere! We were living in a hundred-year-old farmhouse, with lead pipes, lead paint, seamy well water, crumbling outbuildings; storehouses for all sorts of farm pesticides. Moving was out of the question; we had just moved in. Given all these obstacles, how was anyone supposed to get pregnant? My husband said, "That's it! Besides having lead pipes, the water smells like rotten eggs! No more drinking water from this house! I'm buying bottled water!" My cherished twenty-minute siestas in the health club sauna were also abandoned in the first months of marriage: extreme temperatures had adverse effects on a woman's reproductive capacities.

"Honey, get away from the microwave!" I screamed one day. "It's killing your sperm!" Such verbal eruptions were commonplace during these months. Humorous now, they were certainly no laughing matter back then. Months became chopped up fragments of time—a smattering of a few meaningful days separated by wide gaps that were passed over with a loud sigh. The most important days in my womanly cycle were celebrated like birthdays.

I located a temperature chart in the back of a pregnancy book to monitor my most fertile times. I was instructed to track my temperature before rising every day for one month. Well, it didn't happen. Some mornings I forgot to take it, other days I accidentally mismarked the form in my bleary-eyed stupor. So it ended up wadded up like an overgrown spit ball in the trash can. Instead, I purchased a handful of ovulation predictor kits. As the days wore on with obscene slowness, disappointment crept into our daily lives until it became commonplace. We never really had time just to settle leisurely into our new union, like sand sifting through an hourglass.

"Maybe you're trying too hard," one friend suggested.

"It'll happen, you just have to be patient," another said.

"Go away for the weekend and take along a negligée," offered a third. And it continued.

"The only way I could get pregnant, after intercourse, was to stand on my head. Nine months later, Chloe was born."

"John and I had to try for six years before John junior was born. Maybe you both aren't relaxed?"

Some consolation, I thought. Yes, there was some tension. What if our efforts failed? What then? In addition, I started feeling guarded, defensive and agitated, listening to the well-meaning, but deflating, advice.

I decided to purchase half-a-dozen bottles of Robitusin cough syrup after the urging of a friend. "It thins the mucus that helps transport the sperm. Worked for me." So, along with brushing my teeth, taking my vitamin supplements and putting on my makeup, I was slugging Robitusin from a bottle like a wino savoring a last drink.

Extremely active people are suspected of being less likely to conceive than not so active types.[3] My husband, a triathlete, pedaled miles on his road bike, swam laps at lunch every day, and ran ten, twenty miles a week. That had to stop. "Charlie, it says here that overly active people have a decreased sperm count. Marathon runners, especially. And they've proven that sitting on a hard bicycle seat can lower your count. How about laying off for a while? Especially the cycling." He rolled his eyes. It gave me, on the other hand, the excuse to put off exercise that I'd been searching for my entire life. For the first time, without hesitation or guilt, I said, "No, haven't been to the gym this week."

I decided to try some herbal therapy to help us conceive, and, with some in-store searching, found exactly what I was looking for in a local mystic shop: two bottles not even three inches high—a bottle of nutmeg oil and one of rose-geranium oil. Selling exotic scented candles, new age books, crystals of all sizes and shapes, dozens of varieties of incense, tarot cards and the oils I sought, which promised to increase a woman's fertility, the shop was the type of boutique my husband wouldn't be caught dead in. So I went alone. The label on the bottle of nutmeg oil instructed: apply directly to hips, thighs, and pelvis. And I was supposed to add three to four drops of the rose-geranium oil to a warm bath. I routinely added seven or eight. More is better, I reasoned.

I began integrating both herbs into my daily habits. And people were starting to notice.

"What's that smell?" a close associate at work asked. Over time, she became my confidante. "It smells like pumpkin bread."

I knew immediately what the smell was.

"I don't smell anything," I answered.

"It's coming from you," she said, after making a closer inspection.

"OK, OK, it's me. What's the big deal?"

"What's gotten into you?"

"Oh, it's just that I'm a little sensitive these days," I replied.

"More than usual?"

Apparently, my mood swings were obvious at the workplace. I was definitely an emotional wreck—hopeful, on the peak days of my cycle; a dredged up, drowned rat, after the discouraging results.

"No luck yet?" my coworker guessed.

"No luck."

"Hey, keep trying. Look how long it took Sharon and Mike."

"Gee, thanks. I'll try to keep that in mind." I recall pacing around her office. "It's just that I want more from life. Something else besides dog food going for me. I want a family to go home to at the end of a day. I want a rich, full, meaningful life."

She was a good friend, unselfishly listening to my endless wants. Shifting in her chair, she said "I know," and then took another inspecting sniff.

"The other thing that gets me. My life feels like it's been turned upside down yet Charlie, on the other hand, goes into work, comes home, offers encouragement and does the same thing all over again the next day. I'm ready to explode, he's so together."

"My mother said it was always the quiet ones you had to watch. Maybe he's in denial."

With that, we closed our discussion, and I felt a sense of relief for skirting the reason I smelled like a holiday dessert.

Our marriage had changed everything and had changed nothing. I continued to work for a major manufacturer of pet foods and cereal, just as I had done before meeting my husband. When the baby came, that would be an issue we'd have to discuss. As far as I was concerned, I was ready for a new challenge, a challenge like no other, a challenge that only mothering would bring.

Night after night I continued to bathe in the rose-geranium oil. One particular night it was 10 P.M. when I finally climbed into bed. My husband was rudely awakened from the first stages of what was intended to be a sound night's sleep.

"AAH, chuuu! AAH, chuuu! AAH, chuuu! AAH, chuuu! AAH, chuuu!"

Five sneezes in a row. My husband, though athletic, suffered from persistent allergies.

"What's wrong, honey?" I asked as I snuggled closer.

"Something smells like flowers. Have you got something on?"

"No," I lied. "Why would I have perfume on when I'm going to bed?"

"AAH, chuuu! AAH, chuuu! AAH, chuuu! AAH, chuuu! Have you seen my allergy medicine?" he asked, between sneezes.

"It's on your dresser."

He rooted around among the paper clips, crumbled neck ties, parking receipts and match books.

"AAH, chuuu!"

And so it went into the night...until I reluctantly got up, very quietly, to rinse off.

Some things are better left unsaid.

KEEP YOUR SEX LIFE SPONTANEOUS AND FUN

Until now, I felt more than a little uncomfortable saying the word, "sperm." In fact, I don't think I'd spoken it aloud more than once since sex education class in junior high school. Now, sperm, egg, intercourse, mucus, erection and period were as much a part of my vocabulary as working, house, car, shopping, groceries and dishes. I then put all these new terms in the proper perspective, there was a little bit of advice in a woman's magazine—keep your sex life spontaneous and fun. Fun? Charlie and I both found it difficult to relax, much less have fun. "Charlie can you come home right now? ...Have your secretary cancel your meeting...It's time!" With that, my husband would race home, strip off his tie and jacket, jump into bed and we'd begin; then up, re-dress, comb hair, straighten tie, peck on the cheek, pat the dog, and out the door. To finish the fifty-mile round trip before his next meeting, my husband had to haul. One day, he confided that after one of our "encounters" he looked down during a meeting and noticed that he was wearing one brown sock and one black. I wondered if one day he'd put his pants on backwards. It was anything but a spontaneously sensual experience.

Though enthusiastic at first, I quickly tired of researching the subject. "Charlie, it says in this book that the success rate for pregnancy is only 14 percent in healthy, normal couples."[3] It said something else, of course, in another book, and something else again in another. Sometimes, I decided, less really is more.

"It says that even then, pregnancy can take up to a year."

"Don't worry," he said, as we lay down in bed. I was too wound-up to sleep. "Everything will be all right. Wait and see."

I came to appreciate my husband and recognize his optimism as a blessing. He could wipe the slate clean from one day to the next: yesterday's failings were tomorrow's triumphs. My mind, on the other hand, was plagued with constant nagging worry. I fell asleep envying him.

At work, I felt some explanation was necessary for my erratic behavior, my extended, off-the-corporate-grounds lunch hours, and an overall fuzzy ability to concentrate. In this capacity, I felt much like a television set that sometimes got good reception and sometimes got nothing but static. I announced that we had decided to seek medical help to assist us in our endeavor. One unproductive month had turned into six. Besides, I had read that couples over thirty-five, when complications and potential problems statistically rise, should seek such help. Our intimate plans were open for full scrutiny.

THE WORDS OF THE FERTILITY SPECIALIST

"Charlie..honey...something's wrong...are you awake...you've got to take me to the hospital...I can hardly stand up...hurry!"

Before we made our first doctor's visit to seek help, excruciating abdominal pains awakened me in the middle of the night. Endometriosis was the diagnosis.

"What?" I said to the doctor. "You must be kidding?" This came on with no warning, out of no where.

"You're lucky," said Dr. Kalashain. "You have a mild case. Some women have it so severely that it affects their ability to conceive."

After recovering from this set back, I was more determined than ever to get in and talk about our fertility plans. So I made an appointment with the same doctor who had treated me for the endometriosis, who was also a well-liked fertility specialist.

"Can you send over your records?" asked the doctor. My gynecological history had been a crossword puzzle. Every time my insurance carrier changed, I had to switch doctors. All of them, until now, had been men, and I had dreaded my visits to them. During all those years, I'd wondered how a man could understand a woman's body or a woman's feelings about her body? So, Dr. Kalashain, a dark-skinned, soft-spoken, unassuming woman from India, with long fine hair, was to be my hero. She reminded me of a deer in the woods. She was instinctively gentle. My previous male doctors, by comparison, were buzzards—prodding, picking, poking insensitively. I was happy to see them collectively go.

At my insistence, the doctor made room for me in her already cramped schedule.

"I need to review your history. Have you had some surgery?" she asked during my initial exam.

"Is there something wrong?"

"I'm not sure. I need to have your records in front of me," she said.

It was a late winter day, with big snowflakes swirling in the air, when the doctor's office phoned to tell me the findings. Doctor Kalashain was on the line.

"Betsy, I've reviewed your records, along with your exam. It appears as if you had laser surgery three years ago for some precancerous cells. As a result, unfortunately, you also lost some cervical cells that help in the production of mucus. The rest of your exam and history was normal."

It sounded as if she was asking for confirmation, so I replied, "Yes. But what does that have to do with anything? The doctor who performed that operation told me that it would have no effect on my fertility. I asked him point blank."

"He was..." Her calming voice trailed off before finishing her sentence. Mistaken, I thought to myself. That's what she wanted to say, he was mistaken.

She began her sentence again, "You needed some type of treatment, but I would have handled it differently." How diplomatically put, I thought. "Mucus is essential in the transportation of sperm—there's not enough of it for you and your husband to conceive naturally. I recommend you come in again at the beginning of your next cycle. We'll run some more tests and go from there. But you'll need to be artificially inseminated."

This was a bad dream. Artificially inseminated sounded so unnatural. I sobbed, then lay down to rest, and waited for my husband to come home from work. I felt minor relief in the comfort of the pillow, though it seemed to be the only softness left in a hardening world. In the days to follow, I learned what being artificially inseminated involved. And though it offered us a ray of hope, it also meant more anxiety and possibly more pain.

Meanwhile, I had been attending a string of baby showers. Everyone was expecting except me, and they all seemed so young. Some showers were held for women that I knew well, others for those I hardly associated with. With the event of a birth, boundaries of friendships were enlarged. "Now, who's this one for?" I'd ask of another friend who had also been corralled into attending.

I went to most showers, at first, but this latest piece of news rendered me helpless. I couldn't, and wouldn't, attend any more. I just didn't have the resolve. Maybe I'd go again when I was stronger. The joy I felt when shopping for the outfits that until a few weeks before had seemed so irresistibly cute, was quickly evaporating.

After the initial news about needing to be artificially inseminated, I made weekly visits to the doctor's office for the next month to continue my medical workup. I was on a first name basis with all the staff: Candice, Ann, Ellie, Margaret—I knew them all. As time went on, most consoled me the only way they knew, by touching my shoulder on the way out, and saying "Maybe next time. Think positive." I had blood drawn, hormone levels checked, thyroid tests performed and numerous private in-office consultations. And, visits for the inseminations.

Typically, after our orchestrated encounters, I'd run to the doctor's office in order to arrive within the thirty-minute time frame dictated by the nurse for best results. Getting there in this window of opportunity was no small feat. "Out of my way," I'd yell at slower drivers, while the tiny bottle of sperm was kept cradled in my bra, like a babe. The idea was to keep the cargo warm, alive and swimming. "Swim you little sperm, swim!" I kept thinking. On my trips I wondered how many of them had died and how many of them were still alive and doing their thing. While I was changing lanes, being verbally abusive to other drivers or grossly exceeding the speed limit, I felt strangely connected to pregnancy by the urgency of it all. I realized that if the road to the doctor's office was blocked with highway construction, it could mean another twenty eight days to fret. To drift. To daydream.

My mind was also free to concoct a scenario should a police officer pull me over for speeding. I was a woman in labor, driving alone. I kept a pillow readied in the back seat should I need to quickly stuff it up my dress in the event I was pulled over. I wasn't so sure that an officer of the law would be as lenient if I presented him or her with a tiny glass vial tucked into my brassiere.

Once outside the medical building my routine was always the same: screech up to the valet parking, hope that I didn't run up onto the curb, remember to yank the car into park, jump out, leaving the car running.

"There must be some other way to keep the sperm alive longer," I anxiously said to the nurse, completely frustrated from one too many reckless episodes.

"My husband and I are practically killing ourselves trying to get it here in time."

"Well, is your husband's office closer than your home?" she asked.

"Yes, quite a bit closer, why?"

"Some men go into the men's room on their lunch hours."

When presented with this option, my husband cringed. We'd leave it as it was.

It wasn't long before the doctor's waiting room became a torture chamber. It was always overflowing with some form of motherhood—either due-any-day-now expectant moms, or just-given-birth moms holding teeny infants. "When are you due?" "How old is your baby?" "She's adorable. Is she your only one?" was the chitchat of the day. At first, I did much of the asking, but as time dragged on, the chatter wore on my nerves like wet sand inside my swimming suit. It seemed to me that the women trying to conceive should be separated from those who were already mothers, like separating the heifers from the cows.

I carried the book on getting pregnant around with me like a bible. I read it in the waiting room for distraction, and reread it at home for information. Then I'd read it again. I circled the most important parts in red ink. One particularly useful instruction, for a woman receiving inseminations like me, was to lie still in a quiet environment for several hours after the procedure. And I made every effort to do so. Usually this meant taking an afternoon off from work. The days away, though, were adding up. I was feeling the increasing pressure of accountability.

To Do or Not To Do Fertility Drugs

Who hasn't watched the news or read about some couple with quintuplets having been on fertility drugs? Their lives were suddenly turned upside down into endless tasks of diapering, feeding and bathing many more lives than they had previously planned. My husband was more reluctant than I to include these drugs in our prescribed treatment.

"What if you have triplets?" he asked one night at dinner between bites of linguini in clam sauce. "Let's hope not," I said. I'd read that anywhere from 10 to 25 percent of such births were multiples. "Dr. Kalashain said she wants to watch me closely so I don't start making too many eggs." So that I didn't hy-per-stim-u-late, as she explained in her broken English accent. "All that means for me is more trips to the doctor—about every other day."

Clomid, Pergonal, Metrodin, Profasi—all major drugs produced and prescribed in this country, most with side effects ranging from mild to more severe: nervous tension (who needed more of that?), fatigue, hot flashes, nausea, bloating and ovarian enlargement. I began taking Clomid tablets, rather than my choice, Pergonal. Though the success rate is higher with Pergonal, an injectable drug that induces ovulation in 90 percent of the women who take it, our insurance company's policy was for a patient to begin with Clomid, a drug that normally takes longer to work. With Pergonal, about 50 percent of women become pregnant within six months of starting to use it. If that was the couple's only problem.[4]

"I've been reading the literature about infertility in the waiting room," I said, "and I'd like your opinion on performing a laparoscopy, right away." I wanted the doctor to accelerate her timetable. "Shouldn't we be looking inside, too, to make sure nothing is wrong?" Though this was obviously a more invasive procedure than the administration of drugs, she agreed. "Right now, we're scheduling surgery into the end of next month."

"Can't you please squeeze me in sooner?"

"I'll see what I can do."

The test results came back fine. Positive news! All my female organs were where they should have been. My heart was on my sleeve.

But by then, my husband and I were emotionally depleted.

He asked me, "Are you sure you want to go on with this?"

I hesitated. "Sure, I'm sure. Aren't you?"

"I can't stand giving you those shots. And the bills are starting to pile up," he said. What are our chances? Have you asked the doctor?"

We were on a bus ride, and both of us wanted off.

He was right. Our finances had been tampered with, and I feared the stinging shots more than he. We needed to re-evaluate the situation and make a long range plan. The short-term one wasn't working.

While seated in Doctor Kalashain's office, I asked her to lay it on the line: "What are our chances, doctor?"

She opened the manila folder bulging with our accumulating records and ruffled through the mass of Xeroxed test results. She then paused a minute as if to prepare me, and replied, "I'd say, realistically, 15 percent."

"What about our other options?" I asked nervously. "Like GIFT, or ZIFT, or in vitro? What about a sperm bank?"

She shook her head slightly, "I'm afraid the odds go down."

I looked at her daughter's picture on her credenza. I missed my mother. I wanted her to comfort me as she'd done in my childhood. I trembled, then cried.

The doctor leaned across her imposing black desk to get closer to me, "I'm sorry," she said. Those were the same words the psychologist had spoken two years earlier. In both situations I was handed a Kleenex.

"I would suggest you consider adoption."

[1] Niels Lauersen, Colette Bouchez, *Getting Pregnant*, Ballantine Books, 1991, pp. 164-178, 209.

[2] Ibid., p.79.

[3] Ibid., p.46.

[4] Ibid., p. 272.

CHAPTER 3

The Path to Juan and the Dead End to Wendy

"Look for the silver lining."
—B. G. DeSylva

I LEFT DR. KALASHAIN'S OFFICE AND DROVE HOME IN A STUPOR. WHEN MY husband greeted me after work, I told him of our fate as biological parents even before he took off his jacket. "My stomach hurts and my head is throbbing. Dr. Kalashain recommended we end our treatments and consider adoption." That's how I remember much of that night's conversation. Tidbits of medical prognosis shared with my husband, punctuated by my physical complaints. It didn't take a mystic healer to tell me that my karma was all messed up. At that moment I felt hopeless to think that a child would not be a part of our lives, although deep down a corner of me was relieved that all our agonizing was over.

Until then, Charlie and I had not openly discussed the avenue of adoption, focusing instead on the hope of my becoming pregnant. The thought of adopting had crossed my mind, but it was only an on-again, off-again, whisper. It was an option so foreign to both of us. How could we begin to contemplate something that we knew nothing about?

"Consider adoption," my husband said, more as an affirmation than a question. He walked to the refrigerator and stuck his head inside its frosty door. "I think we should go for it. I don't really want to sink a whole lot of money into further fertility options if they won't work. Adoption might be more of a sure thing."

My husband. A surprising individual. Just when you thought you were getting to know him, he'd throw you a curve ball. Not that adoption was a curve ball. It was how quickly he had come to this decision, that was so out of character. I heard the clink-clank of bottles being knocked together and then he emerged from his exploration of the refrigerator, popped open the can he'd pulled out and took a long drink from the new soda. I was stunned by his overall nonchalance. As long as I'd known him, practically every decision, every act, from the most mundane to the most momentous, had been a thoughtful calculation. Predictability was his calling card: Florsheim loafers worn season after season. His hair had been trimmed by the same barber for over a decade. His life had been one long strategically planned marathon: he excelled in analyzing his competition and in judging when to sprint towards the finish. So to say that I was surprised when he had so quickly suggested adoption would be a major understatement. Obviously, he must have thought about this possibility longer than I had.

The doctor's words were still reverberating in my head. She just told us we couldn't have a child. "Maybe it is what we should do," I answered, "but right now I can't see the forest for the trees." I walked into the living room and sat in the lounger for the remainder of the evening. But the promise of adoption soon became like the promise of heaven. It made the passage of time bearable and healed the hurt. In the welcomed routine of going off to work, cooking suppers and talking with friends, I began to see the silver lining. A tremendous pressure had been lifted from our shoulders, and I considered myself lucky to be married to a person who had enough courage and faith to move ahead.

The Road To Adoption

Adoption, say the experts, is not a substitute for infertility. Couples should be at a place where they can allow time to grieve over their inability to conceive before they go on to adoption, like getting over a failed relationship before plunging right into the next one. It just makes sense. Little by little, somewhere in the healing days following that memorable evening, we heeded the experts' advice. While we both knew we wanted children too much to remain childless, the most difficult decisions now lay ahead of us. Which avenue should we take—domestic or international? "If international," we asked ourselves, "which country, and how should we go about it? Should we go through an agency or through a private source?" During the past year, we had been house-hunting off and on. Renting a hundred-year-old farm house was only a temporary situation. We both had other visions that included a roomy house, one with privacy, a house that would bring some of the outdoors inside. Our real estate agent learned of our wishes for a family quite naturally.

"How many bedrooms are you looking for?" she asked early on.

"Four, ideally. Two as the children's rooms, one master bedroom, and one bedroom for guests."

"Another client of mine is considering adopting a child from Guatemala," she said. "She happens to be an attorney, and is extremely nice. I'm not sure where she is in the process, but why don't you give her a call and see what's involved?"

Little did we know then that eleven months later we'd follow that road and end up holding our precious son.

"In Guatemala, the travel time is short," the attorney told me when I phoned her. "A person has to stay in the country only three days. With some other countries, a person has to stay a week or longer. Sometimes, two trips are required. With a Guatemalan adoption, you can also choose to have the child escorted from that country to your home. My husband and I met with the attorney who deals directly with the agency. He's here in town, which makes it convenient when you have to meet with him. Both he and the agency are reputable."

By the time I hung up the receiver, I knew we were on our way. I liked the idea of seeing a face. Dealing with out-of-town agencies meant long-distance phone conversations, and impersonal written correspondence. After the sterility of cold needles and even colder examining tables, I needed the warmth of a human face.

HOME ADOPTION SHOPPING

Additionally, a coworker of mine referred us to a woman who ran an independent adoption counseling business. For a reasonable fee, Beth counseled would-be adoptive parents on their options. She was not affiliated with any particular agency, so basically, it was one-stop shopping. Instead of our phoning a dozen attorneys and dozens of separate agencies, soliciting referrals, requesting and collecting information, and taking care of lots of other nitty-gritty details, she did much of the homework for us. (In fact, it was a service I would highly recommend for those in the early stages of the adoption process; especially busy two-income couples.)

On the evening she came to visit us, she explained that we had not been married long enough to be eligible for domestic placement of any child—Caucasian or not. At least not by any regional agency she knew of. Two to three years was the minimum requirement. We had been married one. She gave us pertinent literature to keep and review, which listed a few agencies, attorneys and support groups in the area. I remember thinking, while she was seated in our living room, that it seemed like only yesterday that I was a young adult who took precautions to avoid becoming pregnant. I suppose, in hindsight, we could have chosen to wait another year or two to get on a domestic agency's list. And have waited again until all the couples in front of us had their assignments. But we didn't. She informed us that our advancing ages were a consideration primarily in domestic programs. Surprisingly, for some, we were simply over the age limit. Too old at forty. That was frightening.

Beth turned to another possible option—private adoption. She explained it very briefly. In many cases, she told us, for private adoptions to be successful, the prospective parents have to let the pregnant moms know of their existence. That could mean placing an advertisement in as many local and national publications as they feel is necessary to get the job done. It also imposes upon a person the responsibility of becoming familiar with their state's adoption laws and hiring an experienced attorney to handle the legalities.

"What do you think about trying to locate a mother on our own?" I asked my husband after Beth had left. We had crossed out most of the agencies given to us on the handouts even before she had opened the door to leave. He shook his head. "I don't want to do that. It sounds like a lot of work, and I think I would feel more secure going with an established agency. Let's talk about it again tomorrow."

In the meantime, I had requested and received information about the large international adoption programs in China and Russia and learned also that we had not been married long enough to qualify for the international programs in Colombia, Romania and Brazil. Eventually, we ruled out China and Russia because of a variety of personal factors, one of them being the long flights involved to physically get the children. Additionally, we had planned on adopting two children, and most, if not all, the children coming from China were girls. We were hopeful for a boy and a girl of the same race. We felt that it was important for the children to have a commonalty among themselves. More importantly, though, as we continued to search our souls for direction, it mattered less if the children's skin was the same color as our own, and more about trusting our instincts.

Later that night, I thought about what Beth had shared with us, playing it over and over in my mind. Too old for some, not married long enough for most. After all we had gone through, we didn't want to risk anything else. We didn't want to risk losing a domestically adopted child because proper counseling was not done with the biological parents or because somewhere down the line a person had a change of heart. Adoption in another country was final: there would be no curtain calls.

GUATEMALA, HERE WE COME

In the following few days we decided to pursue an adoption involving a Guatemalan child handled by the one agency we had been referred to and contacted. We agreed, in part, because I don't think either of us had the emotional resolve left in us to disagree.

After all the discord of the past six months, we desperately wanted harmony and balance back in our lives. An opportunity to achieve an inner peacefulness drove us forward. Soon our attention turned to understanding fully what procedures were necessary to start the process.

I remember being slightly nervous when we first met with the attorney acting as "middle man" between us and the agency he represented, which was located in New Mexico. We were greeted by a robust man with light brown skin whose office walls were adorned with photos of little cherub faces in various shades of brown. Later, we learned they were some of the Central and South American children he had recently placed with other midwestern families. As it turned out, he himself was raised in the Dominican Republic and was intimately familiar with Central America. I was immediately relieved. He helped us begin to bridge the gap between a privileged, predominately Caucasian society and the Catholicism and mixed superstitious beliefs of a poor third-world Latino community. Long before I held our child, we had burgeoning fears of cruel and insensitive remarks. He or she would be a brown child living in an all-white neighborhood and educated, most likely, within a predominately white school system. For all kinds of reasons, our child would get noticed. We realized we would have to be prepared to help our child face the attention positively. We were apprehensive to say the least. Some self-doubt crept in: could we set an example and guide our child without ever having experienced racial injustice ourselves?

We moved forward on blind faith. The attorney assured us that this agency had a genuine concern for the welfare of the children; its founder was a mother of two Latin American children herself. He also attempted to put our fears to rest by stating that the children coming from that country were normally healthy. During our meeting we had a pleasant surprise: from the time the paperwork was completed, most Guatemalan adoptions took only six months—some shorter, some longer, but basically six months. That was quicker than a nine-month pregnancy! We were again hopeful and very excited. "By April, we'll be busy parents—changing diapers, warming bottles, pushing strollers," we said to ourselves.

PREPARING OURSELVES FOR THE HOME STUDY

I was finding out that other couples and individuals have lamented the amount of paperwork required for international and domestic adoptions, and my feelings were no different. Our agency told us what documents would be needed by Guatemala, among them: current medical check-ups for both of us, including blood tests for HIV; a signed original letter from our attending fertility specialist that attested to our infertility; an F.B.I. fingerprint check; proof of both financial stability and life and medical insurance coverage; a letter from our pastor; three letters of reference, one being from a neighbor; records verifying the payment of our state and federal taxes for the past two years and approved completion of a state-approved home study.

For those unacquainted with a home study, which is an agency's early step in its adoption process, here are the basics. An adoption home study is a written report about you and your family that is based on a series of interviews with a social worker, part of whose job is to help applicants think through their capacity to adopt a child. So to prepare for it you'll need to be aware of your feelings and attitudes about parenthood, because you'll be asked to explain them during the course of the study. You may also be asked other questions, such as: What are your expectations of parenting? How did your interest in adoption evolve? What are the reasons for your childlessness? How has your fertility problem affected self-concepts and your marital relationship? How do you view your lives without children? What do you do for fun? As a couple, what do you argue about and how do you resolve these arguments? How were you raised? What were the good and bad aspects of your life? Obviously, a daunting list of questions if you are not prepared or are not used to expressing yourself to a stranger. A home study is usually completed in a few months, depending on the agencies' requirement and the number of applicants. When a home study is approved, your case is assigned to a particular foreign adoption agency, orphanage, institution or private attorney.

From our agency's document pertaining to this issue, the purpose of the home study interviews is to enable applicants to define and clarify for themselves the crucial issues in adoption.

This must be done before you can make a responsible decision to adopt a child. In other words, through this process, the applicants have been able to define and separate their needs from those of the child and be confident that they can gain a healthy measure of satisfaction in meeting the needs of an adopted child. Your willingness and ability to risk and reveal yourselves provides the agency with a means to measure your capacity for adoptive parenting. Adoption cannot be viewed as a substitute if their need is to have a biological child. The couple must be aware that adoptive parenting is different from biological parenting, and they cannot make it the same. To do so, they would have to deny the reality of their infertility and the reality of the child's natural heritage.

We assume that applicants applying to adopt want children and that if they cannot have biological children it is a disappointment. It is not unusual for them to feel hurt, bitter, defective, victimized, incomplete. They must be aware of their feelings and, in some way, have resolved them, before they can invest in the adoption process. Without this awareness, their negative feelings can color or spill over into their relationship with an adoptive child. In our culture, the tendency is to view the giving up of a child as a careless, helpless measure. Applicants must really look at adoption to see if they feel it is a human, natural, okay, thing. Unless the adoptive parents can truly empathize with, and accept the circumstances and motives of the biological parents in their decision to release the child, it will interfere with their task of presenting a positive, realistic picture of the birth parents to their adoptive child. Adoptive parents should be open and comfortable in assisting their child with his or her identity needs.

The option does exist to appeal an unfavorable home study. With our agency, we were told that we had a right to report to the director of social services, who would meet with us to discuss our areas of concern. If, upon review, the director of social services concurs with the findings of the original caseworker, we would have the right to contact the New Mexico Division of Youth and Family Services for further review. Thankfully, that didn't happen. That's not to say we weren't a little apprehensive, because we were. Rumors of nit-picky, stern social workers had reached us. How probing would our social worker be? What if something went wrong? Everyone seemed to be in control of our fate except us.

"Do you think I ought to serve something?" I asked my husband about the upcoming visit. "Maybe the smell of bread baking in the oven would be a nice touch?"

"We're not selling a house. I'm sure he's not going to judge us on the basis of your meal preparation," my husband replied.

"Do you think the house looks clean enough?" I persisted. "What do you think he'll say when he learns we're only renting a house?"

"We'll just have to wait and see."

"How do you think we ought to dress?"

"Like we always do," my husband eventually said.

I thought about what that could mean. Probably a pair of jeans and one of his favorite t-shirts—maybe the faded Rolling Stones t-shirt with the long red protruding tongue on its front.

We met with our assigned social worker, who happened to be a man, in late January: a time of the year when it's easy to bundle yourself up physically and emotionally; a time for hibernation. Charlie chose his best good-fitting shirt, and I spritzed myself with my favorite perfume.

Prior to this visit, we had been informed over the phone that we would each need to prepare autobiographies and have them ready for the initial visit. "Hmmmmm...autobiography," I recall thinking. I had already painfully written my personal ad manifesto. If I had as much trouble writing the autobiography as I'd had with that, well, then, we might as well postpone his visit until the next century.

"The social worker said we have to write our autobiographies before his first visit," I said to my husband.

"What does he mean by that?"

"An autobiography. You know. Didn't you write one in high school like everyone else?" I teased.

"Yeah, but that was twenty-five years ago." He groaned out loud, emitting a sound like air being let go from a tire.

"My sentiments exactly. But we've got to do it."

My husband took off his glasses and rubbed his eyes roughly as he did when he was extremely tired. This time, I interpreted it as a sign of his mounting anxiety.

"How long does it need to be?"

"He didn't say."

"What are we supposed to talk about?"

"I guess that's part of the challenge," I said.

We had only one week to convince a stranger that we would be suitable parents in five hundred well-chosen words or less, a limit we had set for ourselves. My husband's initial hysteria passed and he looked at the assignment like a jigsaw puzzle, examining one piece of his life at a time.

He handed me the results:

I was born December 21, 1951. That was in the days when mother and child spent a week in the hospital recuperating, so that is where I spent my first Christmas. My mother said that they brought me out to her in a Christmas stocking. I am the oldest of three children. My parents have been married for forty-five years. I would describe their marriage as loving, caring, sharing and adventuresome. From them, I have learned that you only get out of something what you put into it. Also, when you make it through the crisis times, like family tragedy, sickness, or financial problems, that serves to strengthen the bonds. Some of my earliest memories include my father reading the Sunday comics to me. I insisted that he read every one, even those not the least bit funny; visiting my grandfather, who lived in the country; and watching westerns with my dad.

Both of my parents grew up during the Depression. Maybe that's why they always wanted a better life for their children. My father received three Purple Hearts and two Bronze Stars in World War II. My mother is outgoing, talkative, athletic and creative. Conversely, my father is quiet, though funny, unselfish and hardworking. He seemingly never got sick and always made it into work, even in the worst snowstorms. Our family gatherings always included my maternal grandparents. My grandmother has been one of my personal heroes. She raised two daughters alone during the Depression. Her arthritis was severe and her hands badly crippled until the time she passed away. But she never complained or sought pity. She was always cheerful, her concern always for others.

My best experience in school was breaking the school two-mile record in track. (As a freshman, I could barely run a quarter mile because of my severe asthma). Some of my fondest memories as a child are of roaming the woods behind my house with my friends Donald, Russ, Louie and others.

I knew my wife a little over two years when we were married. We met through her ad in the paper. It may seem like a strange way to meet someone. But when you're in your late thirties, and want someone who is not a couch potato, likes to do different things, loves the outdoors—water and mountains—and will also drive your car to your family reunion two hundred miles away because you want to ride your bike there, it's not so strange. To look for a person who gets as excited over Christmas and birthdays as a child; someone who thinks with the left side of her brain because you already use your right side too much; someone who will challenge you to be a better person; and you then find that person, it's not strange at all. I consider it fortunate.

I welled up with emotion. It was so poignant. As it turned out, this dreaded assignment turned into a revealing personal odyssey, for us as individuals, and for us as a couple. I learned more about my husband in his telling portrait than months of daily ordinary living would have revealed. Somewhere between the regularity of, "How was your day at work?" and "It's time!" the essence of our lives had been snuffed out. This autobiographical concept was a good thing.

As for me, my numerous initial attempts were wadded up failures that filled the wastebasket to the rim, feeble attempts to pick a handful of flowers from a field of experiences. I went over the stories again and again, until I finally picked a representative collection of them: my Norman Rockwellish upbringing and a childhood spent living on a dead-end street, a street that huddled our neighbors together like eggs in a nest; joining Girls Scouts; playing kick ball; painting murals; earning straight A's in school; crunching into a fine, unblemished, red delicious apple plucked from a heavy tree during an equally unblemished Autumn day. In addition, I wrote about work, hobbies, play, and love...and the loss of my mother.

WHEN THE SOCIAL WORKER CAME CALLING

It was a Wednesday night when our social worker came over. I remember it well. He insisted we call him by his first name, though somehow I thought we should usher him in as "your highness," or "gracious one." I read his business card as he extended his hand. Simply: *Michael Carpenter, L.C.S.W., International/Domestic Adoption Services*

"Please come in and have a seat."

As our social worker took off his coat and handed it to my husband, the wafting aroma of my perfume must have hit his nostrils.

"Something sure smells good," he said with a partial smile.

So far so good.

He joined us in the living room and a surprising thing occurred. By then, I'd anticipated a scene reminiscent of a Perry Mason episode—my husband and I alternately called to the witness stand to defend our lives, but the interrogation never happened. And another thing—no bells and whistles went off. He didn't object to our rental home, or grab a pair of pristine gloves from his briefcase to search every nook and cranny for lurking dust balls. Actually, there isn't much more to tell; nothing out of the ordinary anyway. What advice do I have for others? Ironically, it's the same advice offered to me during the quest for achieving a pregnancy—relax! Instead, save those worry cells for that first infant feeding.

MOVING RIGHT ALONG TO THE NEXT STEP—A GIRL

Our approved home study was submitted by our agency to our foreign attorney after its authentication by the consulate of Guatemala. Six weeks after we met with our attorney, we turned over to him the other required documents: our birth certificates, our letters of personal reference, two additional affidavits swearing to personal character, and employment verification papers. We paid him, and also paid half of the agency's $18,000 fee.

Just what did our fee pay for and how was it distributed?

No costs were hidden. They were all laid out on the table as follows: about 85 percent of our fee was used to defray average overseas expenses. Specifically, $9,000 was for attorney services and court costs; $2,000 went for "in country" services, such as biological family aid, doctor's evaluation and lab fees, translations of documents, official seals, telephone calls and messenger fees; $700 paid for "in country" staff to meet and assist the adoptive family during their stay, including the salary for an aide; $1,000 went for a donation; and $300 for buying new supplies, including clothing, bottles, formula and medicines. This left $2,000 for the domestic operating expenses, which included the agency fee for our social worker's salary, administration salaries, general liability insurance, fax, postage and shipping expenses. The cost for travel was not included, nor any expenses incurred while in the country. We were additionally responsible for foster care expenses for the three months before the adoption was finalized in Guatemala City.

Now all we had to do was wait.

It was explained that we would be notified when the next assignment was available. We had requested a girl. Most of the children coming from Guatemala were infants, though some toddlers were available. We asked for an infant—though it wasn't important to us that the child be a newborn. Newborns scared my husband. Having a newborn to him was like being in possession of a rare porcelain vase, and with an infant we hoped for quicker attachment. We had done some reading about Reactive Attachment Disorder (RAD), and it was somewhat of a concern for us. Experts characterize this disorder as a cluster of distinct behaviors that appear during the toddler years. These include indiscriminate affection towards strangers; clingy behavior towards caretakers; cruelty to animals or younger children; eating issues; control issues; uncontrolled tantrums; theatrical displays of emotion over minor matters, with an absence of appropriate reaction to injuries; and poor eye contact. Clinging to caretakers can alternate with emotional distancing, particularly when a parent imposes boundaries and limits.

We also wondered how an older child who had heard nothing but Spanish would adapt to an English-speaking household and world. Would there be language delays? And if so, to what extent? (In an effort brush up on his high school Spanish, my husband did buy a collection of tapes entitled, *"Spanish Made Easy,"* but after a week or so of listening to them in the tape deck of his car, he decided that the title was a tad misleading.)

Not even our infertility seemed to drag on as slowly as this waiting contest. This was a different type of torture entirely. Two or three times each week I'd phone our attorney's office, wishing for information about a child for us. I was beginning to feel self-conscious. I even resorted to changing my name once when the secretary took my calls. Then one day, unsolicited, our phone rang at home.

"I've got your daughter's picture in my hands," our attorney said. If you want, I'll drop it in the mail."

"No, no, we'll be by to pick it up," we screamed excitedly.

Later that night, the tiny little face, no bigger than a fingernail, stared out of the 4x5 Polaroid at us. Charlie told me later, when we left the office, that he felt like he had known her forever. I fell in love with her immediately. No hesitancy. Her name was Wendy, and she was six months old.

That was in early March, 1995. In the weeks to follow, we were sent a record of what was known of her parents' medical history.

Ailments like scarlet fever, tuberculosis, drug usage, high blood pressure, seizures, and heart problems were listed as unknowns. In fact, many of the items from the four-page report were checked as unknowns. Then we were asked to check off the abnormalities we would accept in a child. Some of them listed were: a minor eye problem, child abuse, venereal disease, minor or major heart problems, corrective orthopedic problems, cerebral palsy, cystic fibrosis, dental problems, asthma, child neglect, AIDS, Down's Syndrome, hemophilia and ongoing psychological treatment. We checked none.

Weeks passed, and we received no more updates on our little girl.

Meanwhile, I found myself, quite naturally, wanting to know more about her. What were the conditions surrounding her birth? Was she a happy baby? What does she know how to do? Does she have any teeth? Does she sleep through the night? Does she like her bottle warm or cold? What does she like to eat? What kind of schedule is she on? Does she have any siblings? How long has she been in foster care? What's the foster care mother like? When will we travel? Will we meet the foster mom? Or her biological mom? Can I send either of them a letter? Does she have any toys to play with? And on and on.

We made copies of the tiny original photograph and carried them around with us, clutching them like prized jewels. Charlie kept one in his briefcase. I treasured one in my wallet. Others were distributed to out-of-town relatives. Everyone we knew shared in our excitement. I felt like the "typical" new mom. "Isn't she beautiful?" I beamed.

By now, we had mutually decided that once she arrived, I would quit my job and take on the job of stay-at-home mom. We felt that in order to solidify the bonding process, it was important for the new baby to have me around full time. A few more weeks went by, and we became troubled by the lack of further information. Call it intuition, but I felt something was wrong. I was learning that international adoptions could sometimes be filled with holes; that it was not uncommon for lumps of time to pass without hearing from anyone—the agency, the foreign attorney involved in the case, the Internal Naturalization Service, the social worker, our attorney. I also learned that Guatemala celebrated many holidays throughout the year, some different from our own, resulting in the closure of government offices for days, and even weeks, at a time. The courts, for example, were closed every year for approximately three weeks before December 25, and three weeks after.

By mid-April we received the news we'd feared. Wendy's mother had taken her back. In the next few days, we were contacted by our agency and informed that her mother had taken her out of foster care, taken her home, brought her back into the same foster care family's home, and taken her back again. We were devastated. We found little comfort in being told, "This rarely happens." How could we love someone so much before even holding her? But we did.

Then Came Juan

My mother used to tell me as a young girl that behind every cloud was a silver lining. Behind the disappointing loss of Wendy, was another silver lining, a four-month-old boy named Juan.

Our agency didn't have another girl ready for placement after Wendy, and they couldn't give us a definite, or even approximate, time when another girl would become available. Though they had several expectant moms in their counseling program, custom and expense prohibited ultrasound testing, which could determine prior to birth the sex of their developing fetuses. We had another decision to make: wait for another girl to be born, or accept the next assignment, a boy.

Prior to learning that Wendy's biological mom had taken her back, I took the tiny color photo of her, drew it from my purse, and showed it to Rita, the Greek mystic. "When we will get her?" I asked. Rita and I were becoming old friends now. Over the past five years, off and on, I'd sought her advice. I wanted her to look into the future and tell me what she saw. It was she who directed me to write down the desirable qualities I was looking for in a man, and then I met my husband. After she'd told me that she saw me working for a Fortune 500 company in my hometown, before I'd even known about the position in the company I eventually got, I had begun to put a little faith in what she said. When she told me I was promised two children in this lifetime, I believed her. But when she replied, "I hear a boy's voice," I was anything but believing. "But that can't be," I protested. "We've already been assigned this child. It's just a question of when." She flipped over the tarot cards slowly, as if for verification. She shook her head, and repeated, more firmly this time, "I hear a boy's voice. You are promised a boy, then a girl—in that order. You are being protected with the girl. Bless it and release it. Every delay happens for a reason."

It didn't take us long to decide to accept a boy. We would hopefully pursue another adoption, a girl, somewhere down the road. Soon thereafter, we received the envelope. In it, was a photo of our future son. Tearing open a Federal Express envelope to reveal the face of your child is an experience like no other. The closest thing it would approximate, I imagined, would be living on a tropical island with 70 degree trade winds blowing through your hair. It was pure ecstasy.

He was the most precious child I had ever seen, though hardly sprouting any hair. He was an angelic creature. Once his biological mother relinquished him to foster care, she never wavered. We learned that she had three other children besides Juan and was in her twenties. She specified in documents that she wanted her son to be adopted by a couple in the United States, so that he would have a good life.

She must be a strong woman. Poor, perhaps, but brave and loving.

Renaming an Adopted Child

With the acceptance of Juan as our adopted son came the opportunity to consider changing his given name. Almost from the beginning were were filled with questions. Should we as adoptive parents rename our child based upon factors other than personal taste? Would it become an issue later in life when the child was older? Would the child have preferred keeping its birth name? What if that child's name is very different, very ethnic sounding? Is that a good thing? Or a not-so-good thing? Charlie and I decided that the naming or renaming of a child was an awesome responsibility. The final outcome could help to decide a person's fate.

While Juan was a perfectly acceptable name in Guatemala, and in other countries for that matter, here in the United States we felt the name might force our son to stand out rather than fit in. In the end, we did what our founding forefathers did when framing the Constitution: we compromised. We decided that we wanted our son to fit into American culture as easily as possible while keeping some of his birth identity. We also factored in the commonness of a name, partly because the kids from my childhood with more unique names always got picked on. And so did the kids with too many freckles, and kids whose names lent themselves to mocking rhymes. "Matty fatty-two-by-four, couldn't fit through the bathroom door" made life miserable for all the Matthews at my elementary school.

After three solid weeks of perusing five baby books checked out of the library (the names Millard Fillmore and Horace Greeley flashed into my head for some odd reason), two or three heated disagreements, and another compromise, we decided upon the name Michael Wyatt Juan. (Charlie pleaded for the inclusion of Wyatt after his western hero, Wyatt Earp).

A Word of Caution

We also learned that, like some other Guatemalan children up for adoption, Juan was born at home with the assistance of a midwife. Probably in an adobe hut. Probably in the mountains. Probably without running water. Probably without electricity.

In the months that followed, we were faced with making the decision of who would travel to pick up Michael.

"Please be careful when you go to Guatemala," cautioned a friend during the course of an unexpected phone call in July of '95. "I was there for two months this spring, and there were times when I felt a little uneasy walking the streets. But then, again, I wasn't there to pursue an adoption." He, instead, had traveled to Guatemala to appreciate its beauty and culture. Though less familiar than our friend with the country's changing and sometimes volatile political climate, we had read a few of the travel updates cautioning American travelers, and knew about some of the false accusations that were circulating. Nonetheless, we declined the opportunity to have our son escorted to us because that option didn't satisfy the intimate connection we needed. Instead, we decided that Charlie would be the one to go. He desperately wanted the opportunity to bond with our son, since I would be the one taking care of him on a day-to-day basis, happily playing the role of disciplinarian, nursemaid, teacher and companion.

We planned for an early October flight from St. Louis to Houston, then on to Guatemala City. Six months after clutching our son's photo, Charlie boarded a plane with our attorney to travel to Guatemala to pick him up. Our attorney went along for moral support and to facilitate the remaining legal steps necessary to complete the adoption process. Our four-month old infant had now reached the age of ten months. "You'll call me as soon as you get him," I said to my husband as he boarded the plane in St. Louis. I suppose I was unconsciously setting the stage for my role as a parent—giving instructions to do the obvious. "Look both ways before you cross the street; we don't put things like that into our mouths; and it's not nice to hit," I was convinced, were soon to follow.

Upon arrival, the two men were greeted by our agency's guide, Eduardo, a Spanish-speaking taxi driver, errand runner, and overall smoother-over—a man of many talents. I was told he was missing one of his front teeth, and that a few of the others glittered like gold when he smiled. Fortunately for my husband, nothing much needed to be smoothed over, unless a person took into consideration a case of nervous stomach.

Visitors traveling to Guatemala for the purpose of adopting were cautioned to stay within the recognized tourist areas and to avoid going out late at night. The following excerpts from a seventeen-page document given to us by our agency detailed further concerns, and ways of dealing with them:

> Before leaving home, be certain to remove all jewelry, except for your wedding band. Also remove all of your credit cards except for one charge card. Do not speak to strangers on the topic of adoption. When asked why you are traveling to Guatemala, your response should be "to visit the ruins." Prior to receiving your assignment of a child, you should be aware of certain conditions that may be encountered when adopting children from the third-world countries of Central and South

America. Children from Latin countries are generally smaller at birth than those born in the United States. Usually, this is a result of poor prenatal care: however, unless the birth mother was actually starving, the baby should not suffer any lasting damage. Also, children from these countries have been exposed to the high levels of copper. This "exposure" to copper will affect the pigmentation of their skin, creating a darker or reddish hue. When the children come to the United States and no longer have copper in their water or food, their skin tone will gradually change. Another possible concern may be the presence of Mongolian spots. These look like blue-gray bruises on the lower back or buttocks, and are temporary.

Two Men and a Baby

Upon his second day in Guatemala, after numerous anxious phone calls attempting to confirm a definite time, Charlie met our son in the lower-level parking garage of his hotel. After being handed Michael, Charlie, accompanied by the Guatemalan attorney, the foster mom, and our attorney, went up to my husband's room to ease the transition period and to give Charlie an opportunity to learn as much about our new child as time and patience would permit. Our attorney, fluent in Spanish, relayed my questions long distance, via Charlie, to the foster mom. The video tape I later viewed revealed Michael playing happily on the bed while the foster mom cheerfully stood alongside and answered our questions in her native language. "He eats refried beans and bananas. He loves food. Food no problem. He is a very happy baby. He has a bath every day at 11 A.M." Charlie had one hand on the phone talking to me as I was pouring out questions, and one eye on Michael, who was taking in his new surroundings with gusto and keenness. "He's beautiful," Charlie said.

I was still firing off questions when he basically cut me off.

"Gotta go...love you, everyone's leaving. I'll call tomorrow," and click.

In less than an hour, my husband was alone with his feelings and an unfamiliar child. Unfortunately, I did not witness some of those valuable moments, nor were they captured on videotape. Moments like

Michael's first diaper change, the first night of sleep in his hotel crib; his first meal and then his first burp; his second, third, and fourth diaper changes; his second night of sleep and so on. I got the impression that this trip was patterned closely after Three Men and A Baby, but here there were only two men. "A lot of fumbling went on," the attorney told me upon their return. He had gotten an adjoining room to my husband's, I learned. That first night with Michael they communicated on the shared wall in Morse code. One knock meant "Are you doing OK," two knocks, "Can't you quiet that kid down?" and three, "I'm calling the foster mother to come back."

The next morning I awoke feeling rested and exhilarated. I recall thinking that it had been the best sleep I had gotten in eighteen months. Our child was in the safe, though virgin hands, of a new daddy.

"Michael cried a lot during the first night. He was probably scared," Charlie said matter of factly during our next day's conversation. His voice did not give any indication about his frustration with his parental ineptitude. "The attorney and I both tried to hold him, but the only thing that quieted him was sucking on his bottle." (A side note here about our son's bottle—actually the nipple on his bottle. It was like something I had never seen before—until I was directed to sift through the pages of a veterinarian's catalogue. It was as extraordinary as the type of nipple used to feed a goat. Our son had only one in his possession when he came to the United States. When it inevitably tore from one too many feedings, you would have thought the world had come to an end.)

The remainder of their three-day stay generally went very well. My husband became more adept at feeding, changing and comforting our son, though when I met them at the airport Michael was still in his sleeper outfit usually reserved for early morning or bedtime hours. It was approaching 2 P.M. The two men and a baby were the last three off the plane behind two stewardesses and the pilots. I wondered if they purposely left me standing there biting my nails to create a scene of high drama.

Those first minutes are difficult to describe. One moment I was overwhelmed, one moment I was elated, one moment I felt flat. Then I felt everything all at once. You would have thought perhaps that a tearful scene ensued, but it didn't. Maybe it didn't because we were in the middle of the hustle and bustle of people coming here, going there: people of all description preoccupied with dragging their weighty suitcases off to who knows where; people racing to make one flight or another. But for me, ours was a scene begging to be played in slow motion. My husband looked exhausted. It appeared as if he hadn't used his razor in three days, and his hair was uncharacteristically a bit disheveled. Our attorney was encumbered with the tools of his occasional second trade: video camera, mushrooming diaper bag, carryon luggage, baby blanket and stuffed bear. Luckily for all concerned, our son slept the entire time during the return flight.

In the midst of a small circle of onlookers, my husband handed me our son with outstretched arms as though he were handing off a football rather than a baby. With those immortal words, "Honey, I think he needs a diaper change," we were on our way to becoming a new family. When Michael looked at me with his searching, brown, Central American eyes, his skin—brown as chocolate milk—pressed up next to mine, I felt as though I had just given birth, every bit as much as if I had been lying on a delivery table. My soul stirred deep down inside.

CHAPTER 4

The Chinese Connection

"A journey of a thousand miles begins with a single step."
—Chinese Proverb

ACCORDING TO THE NATIONAL COUNCIL FOR ADOPTION, BETWEEN ONE million and two million families in the United States are waiting to adopt a healthy infant. That demand greatly outnumbers the approximately one hundred thousand infants and children who are available in this country each year through public adoption. As a result, prospective parents must either wait an average of two and a half years, follow the route of private adoption or look abroad. The International Concerns Committee acknowledged over nine thousand international adoptions in 1995. Guatemala, the Dominican Republic, Mexico, Russia, Ecuador, Peru, Honduras, Romania, Bulgaria, India, Korea, Columbia and Paraguay are some of the countries that are permitting, or have permitted, adoptions.

How does a person decide which country to choose when contemplating a foreign adoption? Is statistical information about the number of placements all you need to make a good decision? What about referrals from friends? What factors do you consider—the length of time to get a child, a child's age or availability of gender? How large a role should the type of care a child is receiving play in influencing your decision? What about cost variances, differences in the length of stay, and safety while traveling? What about prenatal care for biological mothers? If a mother isn't receiving any, should a person discount that option? How important is similar skin color? And what about the varying requirements for each country? Are you too old to adopt in a particular country? Have you been married long enough? What are your options if you're a single parent? And what about religious affiliations? Should inherent cultural differences be an influential factor? Should a person become familiar with a country's attitude toward foreign adoptions? Does it help to know a country's rate for alcoholism, AIDS and drug usage? The list of such questions can be overwhelming.

When many of the parents I corresponded with had narrowed their choices to one or two countries, it was often an instinctual feeling that determined their final selection.

In 1995, 2,130 children were brought to their new homes here in the United States from mainland China. The most populated country in the world—1.2 billion people call it home. China lies over seven thousand miles from the western coast of the United States. It's a country whose traditions have brought us age-old proverbs, fortune cookies, and sweet-and-sour pork; a country whose culture teaches self-reliance and the Confucian virtues of thrift, discipline, industriousness, family cohesion and reverence for education.

To Sharon, who was one of five siblings, and to many other parents, it was a country that offered them the dream of a lifetime. She remembered the events that helped shape the couple's future with children. "My husband and I had informally agreed not to have kids. When I turned thirty-six, I had a change of heart. Things got difficult for awhile. My husband had two children from a previous marriage, and he had allowed them to be adopted by his ex-wife's second husband. My husband always regretted this," she added, "and was afraid to let another child into his heart."

After much time, discussion, and soul searching, her husband opened up to the idea of being a father again. By then, Sharon was thirty-nine and staying pregnant was proving to be more difficult than she had imagined. She easily became pregnant, but suffered her first miscarriage six weeks later. After a short break for recovery and grieving, they tried again without success. Then, as Sharon described it, they got hooked into the infertility loop, with "tests, tests and more tests!" Surgery was necessary due to fibroids and polyps, and Sharon and her husband also tried hormonal therapy and temperature charts. She experienced one more pregnancy and another miscarriage shortly thereafter. In addition, Sharon said, "I began to resent the fact that my husband had fathered two children. I don't think he really understood how hard this was on me, though he really mourned the loss of those two pregnancies." Then she underwent more tests, more ultrasounds, and more shots. Nothing was working.

Besides the medical treatments, there was also abundant advice from well-meaning friends on how to achieve a pregnancy. She recalled some of the most memorable, "Relax, get drunk, go away for the weekend. Stand on your head. Keep your legs in the air for forty-five minutes. Adopt, and then you'll get pregnant!" After both Sharon and her husband had been poked, prodded, invaded and tested for months, their sex life was shot. "Too much pressure," Sharon said, "and needing to have sex at certain times. I couldn't understand what was wrong with me." She was either sad about the fact it didn't work on a particular month, or cautiously optimistic about being able to try again. Then they were told it was time to start thinking about moving to the next step. Deciding to take a couple of months off to reassess their situation, they both came to the conclusion that what they wanted most was to be parents. The pregnancy part of the experience was not as critical as having the chance to raise and love a child.

We started our search for an adoption path with a seminar sponsored by the local infertility network chapter. It was a day-long workshop with agency representatives, lawyers, biological parents, adoptive parents and adopted children. At that point we weren't exactly sure how to proceed, though we knew that because of our ages (I was forty-one, and William was forty-four), our chances of getting a healthy Caucasian baby were pretty slim. We were also extremely uncomfortable with the legal situation surrounding domestic adoption. We had spent quite a lot of money on the infertility treatments and needed to be sure that the money we invested in the adoption would produce the desired result. We didn't have unlimited funds and felt the risk of a birth mother changing her mind was too great. We decided to check out four agencies and explore the possibility of special needs or international adoption.

Sharon and William spent the next two months attending orientation seminars put on by the four agencies for international adoption they had selected. Very early on, they leaned toward China, primarily because they wanted a girl. They also considered Russia and Romania, but were uncomfortable with the political conditions there. China seemed the best fit for their situation.

When they decided upon China, three of their four original agencies were still under consideration. One agency was immediately eliminated because of its inexperience. Another agency seemed to be having financial problems. Dillon International was their eventual choice, mainly because of its reputation with Korean adoptions.

Our daughter, Anita, is twenty-one months old legally, twenty-eight months old biologically. There was a problem with the paperwork in China and they had the wrong birth date on her papers. She was born in the same month that William and I decided to pursue adoption. This is just one reason I am so sure that this was meant to be. Anita needed a mom and dad, and we needed a daughter. William was forty-five and I was forty-two the day we met our daughter. The process took nine months from the time we started the paperwork with Dillon until the day we met her.

A Deaf Couple's Story

Paula and George, a deaf couple living in the Midwest, also had to consider their ages as determining factors when deciding which avenue to take to begin their family. Paula's familiarity with other family members that had adopted internationally initially led her to seek the same path. Though their first assignment fell through, leaving them broken hearted, their perseverance paid off with the successful adoption of their deaf son Alec.

George was over forty when we adopted, while I was in my

mid-thirties. The attitudes toward domestic adoption gave us some mixed feelings, with all of the 'identity crises' of trying to find real parents, or children seeking out their medical history. We felt that would strain our relationship. My family thought the idea of adopting was great, as my sister and her husband had adopted a boy. Their international adoption led us to think of going in that direction. Three years ago, my mother received a call from a family friend whose daughter, living in New Jersey, had seen an advertisement on local television. The agency was looking for adoptive parents of deaf children in the New Jersey and Maryland areas.

Initially, we never received a return phone call from that agency, so we went ahead with our home study with a local agency instead. We gave them all the information we could think of to prove that we were able to care for a child, even with our disabilities. In our home, we showed them devices for the deaf that we depended upon—devices like a flashing signaler that would tell us if the baby was crying or making other noises. We also had a decoder for closed caption TV, a signal for the door bell, a smoke alert alarm, and a phone flasher.

With no phone call from the agency in Baltimore, we felt like we should go ahead with our planned three-week vacation. When we returned home, there were two urgent phone calls! It turned out that the agency had found a baby from Europe who was deaf and they wanted to know if we would be interested in him. We said, 'yes', and proceeded with the paperwork. Six months later, in November, we received the medical report on the baby. Unfortunately, the baby had severe health problems. It was a hard decision to accept or reject him, but ultimately, we turned the assignment down.

Our lives were strengthened during the Thanksgiving and Christmas holidays by being around our loved ones. They gave us their support, and it made us decide to could go ahead and resume the adoption process. In January, we told Adoption Together, Inc. (A.T.I.) in Baltimore to go ahead and find us another deaf child. We decided a deaf child would be fun to have. We could share the experiences we were most familiar with. The answer came by early February. There were several deaf Chinese children available. So we did our homework to study another country. More paperwork was dealt with which caused some stress, as everything had to be revised to fit a different country's rulings! Then one day a packet arrived by overnight mail. It offered four children for adoption. Because of Chinese law, we were allowed only one child per adoption. We selected the only boy.

Waiting eagerly to get the call to go in September, as promised, Paula and George filled their time with thoughts of what their lives would soon be like. They believe Alec was abandoned at eleven months because of his deafness. After being found, he was placed in an orphanage. The couple decided that they would eventually tell their son the truth about his abandonment. After three delays, the couple left for China in late October, 1995. Paula said she never dreamed of going to the Far East in their lives! Filled with mixed feelings of how they were going to deal with a new child who was already three-and-a-half, they were accompanied by a friend who lent moral support, as well as aided in translations and legal proceedings. Once in China, they devoted some extra time before getting their son to visiting the Great Wall, the Forbidden City, the Summer Palace, and the main tourist areas in Beijing.

We went through so much paper work. To our surprise, Alec was waiting for us at the Notary Office in Wuxi, China. It was a surprise that took our breath away...no tears, just joy. My family and George's family didn't care what nationality Alec was. They would give him their love and support under any circumstances. If the public gives us trouble about him being from a different country, we'll tell them that we're happy to have Alec to love.

As Paula described it, her son didn't exhibit much personality when they got him. He was thin and was suffering from an ear infection. By the time they had brought him home in November, though, after a ten-day stay in China, he had put on weight. Now, Alec is described as being active and friendly. Paula and George plan on exposing their son to both American and Chinese culture as he grows up. As Paula put it, "We don't want him deprived of his proud heritage!" At last check, Alec knew over one hundred signs and is currently in preschool for deaf children.

Another couple, Rene and Bob, traveling with the military, remembered that the turning point in their consideration of adoption came after they'd had three biological children. Their faith in God helped them through the difficult, but manageable, concern of how to afford an adoption, and their family and friends fully supported their choice to adopt a child outside of their ethnicity. In fact, their choice was readily and warmly embraced.

My husband and I had always wanted at least four children, but decided that after three cesarean deliveries that we would bring additional children into the family via adoption. My husband is an Air Force officer, and multiracial families in the service are so common that no one gives them a second glance. So many servicemen marry women they meet overseas and bring them back to the states. Also, being Christians and members of a wonderful, supportive church has helped. One lady in our church commented to me the first Sunday we were in church with our daughter, 'It's almost like the whole church had a baby!'

As Christians, we trusted the Lord to provide the financing somehow, or to show us how to finance it. We paid for some expenses out of our savings, took out a line-of-credit and also secured a loan. I've heard all sorts of ways folks finance their adoptions. You do what you must to achieve your goal.

Because we're an Air Force family, we were constantly moving. It was never the right time to pursue adoption—until three summers ago. Knowing that we would be stationed in one place at least three years, we decided to finally look into it. After some thought and prayer, we sent off for some information from Holt International Services in Eugene, Oregon. I'd always been familiar with Holt, as my parents started the process to adopt a child from Korea through Holt when I was only six years old. That was more than thirty years ago. International adoption wasn't the same then as it is today. Unfortunately, due to red tape, the adoption process ceased. I never forgot about Holt and the good work they were doing, as I heard about it often while growing up.

Rene and Bob themselves had intended on applying to adopt from Korea, but upon receiving the information from the Holt agency, discovered that in order to adopt from that country through Holt, they had to either live in a state where that agency had a branch office (which they didn't) or be prepared to adopt a child with moderate-to-major special needs (which, at the time, they were not prepared to do). "This is a rule of the Korean government," Rene explained. "I was so disappointed, but at that moment, the country update guide fell from the Holt information booklet. The first words I saw were: 'Adoption in China is open! We need a lot of families.' That was all we needed to know, and I definitely felt that the Lord was leading us to apply to adopt a minor special needs infant girl from China."

Chinese adoption law requires that only families who already have children can apply to adopt children with special needs, which, of course, was the case with Rene and her husband. They thought that the process would take no more than nine months, if that long. But their adoption had delays. Their home study took much longer than anticipated, due to some unforeseen circumstances, and paperwork glitches. Rene added, "Considering that a family adopting internationally has to satisfy their home state, their home study agency, the international adoption agency, the United States government, and the foreign government, it's a wonder anything gets done!"

She recalled many frustrating times when they thought the adoption would never happen. The process was emotionally hard on their three children, who were ten, nine, and seven, at the time. Prayer and faith helped them manage. Then, ten weeks after they'd sent their dossier to Beijing, to the China Center for Adoption, at 3:15 in the afternoon, their local social worker called with those magic words. Beijing had selected a three-and-a-half month-old baby girl, who was in the Nanning Social Welfare Institute's orphanage. Her health left much to be desired. She suffered from malnutrition, which was evidenced by her sunken eyes and little, if any, hair, and the medical report indicated that, in addition, her right foot turned out. Rene and Bob had decided in the beginning that the child Beijing referred to them was the one the Lord intended them to have. They accepted the medical reports on faith.

Less than two weeks later, Bob had to leave with the Air Force on a ninety-day temporary duty to Riyadh, Saudi Arabia. Tearful goodbyes were said with full knowledge that Rene could be called to bring home their daughter while he was away:

> In mid-November, some friends who were also adopting from Holt traveled to Nanchang China to bring their eight-month-old daughter home. They were able to bring a newer, updated photo of our little girl, whom we had decided to call Tess. What a difference. She had chubby, baby cheeks, finally, and a full head of hair. And she was beautiful! The Lord answered our prayers that she would become and remain healthy and we continued to pray He would keep her safe until we could bring her home.

Two months after receiving their daughter's photo, Rene and Bob received word from their agency that they had been approved to travel. They would soon be heading to Hong Kong, or at least Rene would. Long before that, they had decided that their oldest son, Stan, would accompany Rene on the trip. The return from the trip was on February seventh—five days after Bob was to return home from Saudi Arabia. Rene and Stan left from Minot, North Dakota, for Hong Kong, and joined up with thirteen other families in the agency travel group. "I'll never forget landing in the People's Republic of China," Rene explained. "On our way to the hotel from the airport, our guide announced, 'The babies are already at the hotel and are waiting for you.' The precious little girl I had longed to see for so many weeks was waiting for me!"

Thirty minutes after their arrival at the Qing Shan Hu Hotel in Nanning, Rene's name was called, and a "precious, beautiful and somewhat scared little seven-month-old baby girl was placed in my arms. Tess, at last!" The adoption was finalized the last day of January, and the group spent the remainder of their time, while waiting for the preparation of their girls' passports, in sightseeing, shopping, and getting to know the land from which all the newly adopted daughters had come. The group then flew to Guangzhou, China five days later to do the visa application work at the United States Consulate. Then they flew home. It would be an understatement to say that it was a joyous occasion for Rene to greet her other two children, her mother and her husband, and to place their new daughter in her husband's arms for the first time.

In some cases, with international adoptions, an infant may be suffering from malnutrition, but in time, once in the care of American doctors and surrounded by full-time nurturing, the children begin to thrive. Tess was no different:

> The trip to China was absolutely fantastic! Initially, I was nervous about traveling, having never visited any other country but Canada. The more I spoke with people, however, the more excited I became about the trip. I took our oldest son, Stan, with me. He was just a month short of twelve at the time. We had a wonderful time in Hong Kong and in China. The Chinese people were great, very friendly. We saw and did things a lot of folks may never have the chance to do.
>
> Now that we're home, Tess loves her big brothers and her big sister. They take care of her beautifully, and there has been no jealousy from the older three. Tess is healthy and her right foot does not turn out. Even now, we're contemplating the adoption of a special-needs infant girl from Korea.
>
> As far as continuing her heritage—we want her to learn all about it. We'll learn along with her. To prepare our older three for the adoption, we saw films, read, watched TV—absorbing anything we could find about China. We'll do the same for Tess. In addition, we're members of Families With Children From China and receive their newsletter. It's a marvelous source of help for ideas on how to instill cultural awareness and a pride in one's ethnicity. I've learned that the Chinese New Year is the 'biggie', followed by the Autumn Moon Festival and the Dragon Boat Festival. Everything closes down in China for the Chinese New Year. The children get two weeks off from school, the houses are cleaned and everyone goes visiting. Fireworks are important, you eat special food, people wear new clothes and children get money gifts in little red envelopes. Red is definitely the color for good luck. It's a lot of fun. We're forming a Families With Children From China chapter here in North Dakota, too.

Holt International also sponsors heritage camps in the summer, where children from the age of nine on up to seventeen can go for a week of learning about their culture and have fun while doing it. "Definitely, we'll want her to go to that," Rene added, "when she's older, say, out of high school. We want her to be able to travel back to China someday—hopefully, to the province where she was born."

ONE MAN'S POIGNANT JOURNAL

Next, a detailed account of one married couple's emotional journey through the process of deciding to pursue a Chinese adoption. From Texas, Henry and Lisa explain how they settled upon China and, through his journal, give insight into what many prospective adoptive parents, both married and single, often face: a process of elimination through personal study. Their long-awaited trip is detailed here, offering helpful tips to those individuals who have yet to travel. It's a uniquely introspective account written by a man who courageously reveals himself to us, to his wife, his friends and eventually to his beloved daughter. It's a story full of questions and probing. From a journal Henry kept, he shares the following excerpts:

7/4/94
Brother-in-law and sister-in-law came to visit this weekend. They brought their son, Lisa's nephew. I'm not sure how old he is, maybe six months. He's at the almost-crawling state, and generally has baby food all over his face. Although we've seen him several times since his birth, Lisa fell in love with her nephew this time. More importantly, she fell in love with the idea of getting a baby of our own. I'm still not completely sure. Infants make me nervous. They break easily and poop a lot. But the look in her eyes is unmistakable, baby love and maternal want. Maybe this would help her grow and teach her how to care for more beyond herself. Maybe this is what she really does need.

We're thinking about losing our free time, and about our ages, thirty-six for her, thirty-seven for me. We're also thinking about long hours in the middle of the night, baby sickness and adolescent children wishing they could replace us with better parents. Our own difficulties and self-doubts about growing up are also surfacing. We have learned a lot, though, about love and have more to share.

7/13/94

Lisa and I visited the preacher tonight to talk about having kids or adopting. He said that although it was a huge amount of work and all of our personal lives would be absorbed by raising kids, until we did, we couldn't even imagine the fulfillment they would give us.

8/8/94

We went to our first adoption meeting, held by an adoption agency in Fort Worth. We discussed everything from Paraguayan foster homes (which seemed relatively nice), to the fate of Chinese female infants at orphanages (which have zero resources) who do not get adopted. If they get any illness, they die without treatment. We brought back more information, including pictures of the typical children. We felt very comfortable with this agency.

Surprisingly, the Chinese costs aren't much more than the Paraguayan agency's. We still change our minds two times a day as to whether we want a girl or a boy.

8/10/94

I'm considering the name of our child. One of the adoption books I read suggested you use the kid's first birth name as a middle name.

9/13/94

I stopped at a local bookstore today at lunch. I found a couple of books on the people and land of China and Vietnam. I guess our current choices are:

Paraguay—80 percent chance of being a boy, at a cost of $25,000, with two one-week trips to Paraguay.

China—99.9 percent chance of being a girl, at a cost of $21,000, with one two-week trip to China.

Vietnam—?? chance of a particular sex, at a cost of about $17,000, with no travel recommended because of current conditions.

Lisa really likes the way the hair on oriental infants stands up and looks cute. These fuzzy baby heads will probably lead the decision-making process, but this is as reasonable as any other scheme for choosing a child.

9/20/94

I called another agency to ask them about their Vietnam program: there is a one-to-two year waiting list for infants. While I
was at it, I asked them about the line in their book that dis-
qualified us with them for Chinese adoption: the requirement
that we have a doctor's certificate of infertility. To our knowledge, we're not infertile. That has nothing to do with why we
want to adopt a child. We want to love a child that already needs
love. There is little need in creating another child that needs
love when there is one waiting for us. Anyway, they told me that
infertility is a Chinese requirement for all agencies, but that
China no longer seems to be using this as a filter. In fact, they
are even allowing families with existent children to adopt now.

9/28/94

Since we've always been more interested in adopting than in
pregnancy, we've decided to adopt a Chinese girl.

10/04/94

We went to the meeting held by the agency we selected. It was
great. This agency has made a different approach in China from
the other two agencies we had considered. They came to China
and looked around at various locations until they fell upon an
orphanage in a city named Nanning, in the southeastern
province. At this orphanage, they discovered that the children
who were left there had about a 90 percent mortality rate after
only a few months. Their hearts were inspired to find a way to
help the people at this particular orphanage to do a better job,
and, hopefully, save the lives of some of the children until they
were old enough to be adopted. China requires a three-month
newspaper advertisement for abandoned children in order to try
to find any interested blood-related family member before they
declare the child officially abandoned and available for adoption.

Our newly selected agency did not want to send in medical
help, food, diapers and money from the United States, since
they would become dependent on this, and it might be interrupted by either government. Anyway, they educated, planned
and developed functional methods to help the orphanage workers keep the kids alive. They talked to city leaders and commu-

nity groups and sought help from local suppliers. A network of foster families developed that now takes care of forty infants. Once they arrive at the orphanage, a family takes the baby home and raises it until a new family can come and take it.

10/21/94

We received a letter from our agency today telling us that they received our application and that they will be notifying the home study people. Wow! It's begun.

10/30/94

Most of the dossier is complete. We still need the sheriff's department to send our police clearances, but they've started. We also lack the picture album we must send, and our completed home study, but we just got the home study application yesterday, and it will take a few months for the social worker to 'do' us. We bought a book called *The Father's Almanac* yesterday. It tells me stuff like how to hold, burp and diaper a baby, and so on. I need it.

11/13/94

I found myself crying in church today. I was thinking of the huge circle of people and love that has to exist in order to allow us to adopt this child. God's love is all around. First comes the step of faith that the mother has to take to abandon her child; hoping not only that she not be arrested, but hoping that the child will be taken care of by people she does not know. There are the agency people who started all of this and took the trouble to create the paths we're using to adopt. Then there's the family in China who is willing to take this child and love it for a few months in order to spare its life. If we don't have her birth date, perhaps it will be November 13, the day I first cried for her.

1/05/95

We received our I-171 H form today. This is the form from the International Naturalization Service (INS) that 'preapproves' us to adopt an orphan. This means that the FBI prints came back and that the home study was acceptable. Tomorrow I'll get

copies made and forward them for translation. Once they say
the forms look OK, I can proceed to get state, and then Chinese
authentication. Thank you, God. I'm excited!

1/14/95

Today, we got a letter saying everything is fine and we may
begin the authentication procedure.

1/20/95

On Wednesday, I flew to Austin and rented a car and drove
downtown. I got thirteen documents certified. That means that
for each notarized document, I got a cover letter with the Seal
of the State of Texas and the signature of the Secretary of State.
On Thursday, I took these documents and flew to Houston,
rented a car, and drove to the Chinese consulate. There they
were authenticated. That means that a Chinese bureaucrat put
his seal on the papers saying that the person who signed the
certification was who he said he was. All of this cost $520,
cash. Now, as soon as our agency finishes translating everything and messing around with paper, our dossier will finally
be sent off to China for approval. Oy vey. I am a little thrilled
at how close it's getting.

In early February, a major misunderstanding erupted surrounding
one of the couple's requirements. Specifically, it pertained to China's
requirement that a couple be infertile, a requirement that the couple had
been told was being relaxed. Henry noted that what is not reflected in
his following letter is how hopeless, sad and heartbroken they were.

To Whom It May Concern:
    This is to certify that Henry and Lisa have no intentions of
achieving pregnancy, either now or at any time in the future.
We have been married for twelve years without pregnancy. Lisa
has severe headaches that must be treated with drugs, which
would harm a developing fetus. If her headaches go without
treatment, she is in significant pain for extended periods of
time. Because of this we use birth control regularly and will not
allow a pregnancy. Our family doctor is not willing to write a

letter stating that it is inadvisable for my wife to become pregnant because of her headaches. He thinks it is a good idea that she have some other extensive testing done, which might reveal she has Lupus, which would indicate no pregnancy.[1]

Our family doctor is unwilling to give me a vasectomy and write a letter of infertility for this purpose (although he was previously receptive to the idea.) What are our options now? What is likely to happen if our dossier is processed "as-is?" In the event this puts us into a "special needs" situation, what are the procedures involved, and what happens if we choose to reject the child assigned to us?

Within a month, the couple was notified that they needn't worry; everything would proceed as normal. And it did. In late March they were assigned a child, Yuan. The journal continued:

One week after they'd notified us, the agency called me at work to tell me they had canceled the baby and put us back in the stack for another child. Apparently, she was not a part of their foster care system. They didn't even know who, or where, she was when they contacted us. I wish they would have told us in advance that this type of thing can occur. We wouldn't have started to fall in love with an image. Depression is not a good way to describe our state. In pregnancies, there are miscarriages. This was ours. With God, in all things something wonderful can be found. A different child will be our blessing. We will all be blessed in our togetherness, but it still stinks.

Early in May Henry and Lisa received their second assignment, born or found in August of '94. They also received a medical exam from the orphanage doctor indicating that the baby was healthy, but developmentally delayed and suffering from "not fine" nutrition. Both of these conditions were due to life in a Chinese orphanage. Currently, half of the agency's adoptions involved infants not in the foster care system, though that system was what originally influenced Henry and his wife to select this agency. Now, however, they were too emotionally committed to refuse the child:

5/11/95

I wrote the Chinese consulate to ask them what to do about our visas, which expire in June. We're expected to travel sometime around end the of June or in July.

6/06/95

We received our visa extensions today. They give us an extra month. The consulate also translated her name for us: 'It means she'll be very diligent in every aspect of her life when she grows up.'

Three days later Henry and Lisa were contacted by the agency again. They were informed that their soon-to-be adopted daughter was living at the home of a retired soldier in Guilin and that pictures of her would be available soon. In late August of '95, the couple made final plans to travel to China. They flew to San Francisco from Dallas, and then on to Hong Kong. From there, after a brief stay, they boarded another plane that was headed for Nanning and the orphanage that housed their daughter. While in Hong Kong, their agency held an orientation meeting over breakfast. Henry remembered a suggestion noting the importance of bringing Cheerios for the baby to snack on. They were also instructed to be prepared for everything, and also told to expect changes. "Other than that, if you plan to get a great deal of specific information beyond the written data they have already provided," Henry advised, "plan on having a list of particular questions to ask."

THEIR TRIP FROM HONG KONG TO NANNING

In flight we filled out our People's Republic of China entry forms and health cards, which guarantee hospital care. The airline messages were in both Chinese and horrid English. On the final approach, we could see the dense farmland full of banana trees, rice and sugar cane. The waving grass near the runway reminded me of all the airport scenes from all the assorted Vietnam movies I had seen. I spotted what seemed to be three MIGS of Korean War vintage parked in the weeds. Two water buffalo grazed on an overgrown asphalt basketball court that was right next to the runway.

On the ground and through customs, everyone rushed to get at one of the rusted, broken-down luggage carts outside the terminal. Once Lisa and Henry had their luggage in hand, they pushed their way with other passengers through the entry. At 4:30 P.M., they arrived at their hotel and, with the help of their translator, checked in.

It's standard procedure for foreigners to present their passports as part of their hotel check-in. The room itself was a First Class 1960s model of luxury, complete with a console between the twin beds that had switches for all the lights in the room and for the TV. Considering it wasn't the '60s anymore, the room was in good shape and clean. Then our translator updated our itinerary: we would receive our child tonight at 9:40 P.M.

I became a total basket case for the next hour and a half. I repacked and unpacked and rearranged and fidgeted. I sat in a chair and stared deeply into blank space and tried to figure out why diapers work. Lori napped; I panicked. We decided to meet another couple downstairs for dinner at the hotel restaurant. I was beginning to think clearly by then, and the panic buzz had subsided significantly. As it turned out, this restaurant is very convenient and is very accustomed to adoptive families. Ordering is generally done by pointing to the item on the menu that you want. For those evenings when the baby or you do not feel like a family outing to a restaurant, you can go to the restaurant to order your food and then take it back to the room.

Breakfast at the hotel restaurant was also a great deal of fun. While you could order freshly peeled melons and fruits for breakfast, the traditional fare is Dim Sum. Dim Sum is a meal consisting of a huge variety of steamed meats and vegetables in either rice dumplings or wontons. The waiter walks by with carts of assorted baskets and you point at what you want to try and they place two or three of each of the small items on the table. Sometimes you can tell what is in the items, such as anything wrapped in a steamed wonton. Because the wonton turns clear once steamed you can easily guess what you're getting, such as shrimp with green vegetables and carrot. Tipping is not expected, appreciated or even legal in the People's Republic, so don't confuse the staff by forgetting money on the table. They don't want to have to return money to another careless, bourgeois American.

MEETING THE BABY

After dinner we went back to the room and talked about Chinese political history while we waited for 9:40 P.M. to roll around. At 10:30 P.M. our translator called our room to tell us she was downstairs in the lobby and on her way up with the baby. I use the word 'translator' to refer to the agency representative, but this word is insufficient—facilitator, guide, guardian, expediter, or blessing might be more appropriate. We opened the door and stood in the doorway. Our translator, a well-dressed lady, and a very haggard-looking man in an open shirt holding a baby came down the hall. The baby was Mishael. Mishael is Hebrew for 'one who belongs to God' and I could definitely feel the power of something larger than all of us as she came down the hall to be our child.

As it turns out, the haggard man was the assistant director of the orphanage she had come from. He had personally picked her up from her foster family and carried her here this evening on a six-hour train ride. His shirt was open because she only had the one "diaper" she had been wearing, and he consequently received the 'golden shower' from her on the train.

They came into the room and our translator told us that our new daughter loves congee and rice cereal; that she needed a bath, but they hadn't had time to give her one; and that she preferred men to women. He handed her to me. Then they all left. She had been left in front of the gate of a factory by her birth parents eight or nine hours after being born. She was then taken home and cared for briefly by a lady at the factory, who was legally obliged to leave her at the orphanage. She was taken from the orphanage after eight months and given to a foster family. After living there for four months, she was brought to us. She looked deep into my eyes with a desperate, soul searching inquiry, and began to cry from her very core. I didn't understand either, and so we cried together. She baptized me with a flood of urine as we walked around the room together. It wasn't more than twenty minutes or so until she fell asleep against me from exhaustion. As she lay there on me, sweating, her skin against mine, breathing stuffily from her crying, I was filled with awe, and just a little concerned about the skin problem she seemed to have all over. We were told to expect a minor contagious louse, like scabies. After another thirty minutes of sleep against me, we decided to lay her down, give her a sponge bath, a new diaper and dress her in pajamas. She had been cleaned some, but her smell filled my nostrils all night. This was not the smell of a baby as I knew it. Her smell reminded me of corn-fed duck eggs.

MORE ADOPTION BUSINESS

After meeting with our translator in the lobby after breakfast, we took a ten-minute walk through building hallways, alleys, streets, puddles and who-knows-what else to the Office of Civil Affairs. At the office we signed an "adoption agreement" and various adoption forms. We placed our thumbprints and our daughter's footprints in red ink on assorted papers. We also formally met the gentleman from the evening before. The ultimate purpose of the meeting was to obtain her official Chinese Birth Certificate. There were lots of photo opportunities here, and as a matter of fact, if someone offers that, 'this might be a good opportunity for a photo,' what they probably mean is that it is time to roll out the camera and take a picture, even if you're out of film. We were interviewed together, attested to the fact that we had enough money to raise our new child, and verified that we would not abandon her. Our next step would be to wait. The Nanning paperwork would be ready soon, and then we would head off to Guilin to wait for the passport. Fortunately, our translator was going to arrange for shopping and tourism during our wait.

Two days later, after touring a museum and getting some much needed rest, Henry and Lisa prepared to travel to Guilin by train to meet their daughter's foster family. Henry continued with his observations about traveling with a baby.

> You have to get up a little early to travel with a baby. They need to eat before you go out. They need time to be sociable and friendly to start each new day in a good mood. So, realizing that we needed to finish packing essentials, take care of baby, eat, take care of ourselves, check out of the hotel, take a taxi to the train station, and then take a train ride to our next destination, we got up at 4:30 A.M.

The next morning, when they arrived at the Guilin Sheraton after an uncomfortable, though scenic, train ride, their agency guide informed them that they would not be meeting with the official at the orphanage as planned. The reason? Apparently, the orphanage had previously allowed British film crews to document it without going through the proper government security channels, so Westerners were not being allowed in. Then, since standard practice doesn't warn the foster family that adoptive parents are coming (most families don't have phones anyway), their daughter's foster parents were out shopping at the market, when Henry and Lisa arrived. Only their biological son was home. He prepared tea for them, and they learned of their daughter's nickname, Tien-Tien, which means 'little spot.'

The orphanage selected its foster families based upon several criteria. First of all, the age of the couple was important: they must be retired, but not too old to care for a child. The foster mom in this instance was a retired worker, and the foster dad was a retired soldier. The home must be very clean. There must be no dogs in the house, because dogs carry diseases. And finally, there must be no smoking in the home. The particular couple chosen to care for Misha applied to the program after they heard about it from a worker at the orphanage.

In retrospect, Henry noted that there is very little privacy in China. When traveling, especially with a group, a large proportion of the meals will be taken in public places. When conducting business, even without a group, you travel with others, wait with others, change diapers with others, take tours with others. He detailed his frustrations:

I didn't expect this. Neither Lisa nor myself was prepared for the constantly recurring heavy feeling of having to go out and face yet another unknown experience in China, when all we wanted to do was take care of and experience our baby girl. And we're adventurous travelers. I've traveled unescorted into the mountainous regions in the interior of Mexico at night without a map or any real idea of where I was going. I've chaperoned teenagers to live in tents in Juarez on mission trips. Lisa has been all over Europe. This is not the same.

From Guilin to Guangzhou and Home

After receiving the baby's passport the following day, touring Guilin on Saturday, and resting on Sunday, Henry, Lisa, and Misha departed Guilin for Guangzhou. There, they completed their daughter's physical exam, which was required by the United States Consulate before it would issue an immigration visa for Henry and Lisa's new daughter, who was, of course, a Chinese national. Later in the day, they made their appearance at their consulate and prepared to depart the People's Republic of China. One might expect that arriving back in the United States after being in a foreign country for so long was a wonderful experience, but to Henry, arriving on American soil seemed like just another airport. What were his final thoughts?

I wish we had allotted more time in China so we could have experienced all of the things we wanted at a relaxed and leisurely pace. Since we didn't do that, we spent a lot of time being frustrated by doing too much in too short a time. This was not a vacation. This was becoming new parents to an abandoned child while on an odd and grueling ten-day business trip in a foreign country that could conceivably have gone sour through no fault of our own.

The following message made available on-line might be the answer for how Henry and Lisa and many parents of Chinese daughters can tell their children about the circumstances of their arrival.

Once upon a time, in a land that is far away and is very different from here, a couple had a baby girl. That baby girl was you. All I know about the couple is what I can see in you, and so I guess they were a handsome pair and very bright. Even though they were bright, they were like people everywhere in the world. Sometimes, especially when things get rough, people make mistakes. When they had you, they left you in front of a factory gate where they knew you would be found in the morning. Even though you had to wait without a mommy and daddy for awhile, finally, with the help of many loving people here, and in China, your mother and I found you and brought you home. We love you with all our hearts, and we will never leave you, even if we are poor, if we are angry, if we are sad, or even forever.

[1] Recent medical research indicates that under the right conditions, most women with lupus can get through pregnancy with few, if any, problems and will deliver normal, healthy babies. Robin Dibner, M. D. and Carol Colman, *Lupus Handbook for Women*, Simon & Schuster, 1994, p.123.

CHAPTER 5

To Russia With Love

UNDOUBTEDLY, LARGE NUMBERS OF ADOPTED CHILDREN WHO ARE LIVING IN THE United States were born in the former Soviet Union. Four thousand children were adopted from Russia in 2000 alone. Long before Charlie and I considered adoption for ourselves, we both knew of families who had selected this path as the way to realize their dreams. Today, several Russian states allow adoptions—Belarus, Russia and the Ukraine. It's difficult to generalize about the adoption process for any one country, since the circumstances of the adoptive parents or individual, the agency used, and the area of the country the adopted child is from are so unique.

Currently, there are several active programs in the Ukraine, each of them with slightly different requirements. For example, one of them, International Adoption Resource, has toddlers at least fourteen months of age, sibling groups, and children with mild to moderate health issues. The agency states that upon arrival, adoptive parents will be shown several children who meet their requirements. While in the Ukraine, they will decide which child to adopt. The agency further states that two trips are required during the adoption process, and that adoptive parents may be up to sixty years of age. Dillon International, Cradle of Hope and Commonwealth Adoptions International are among other agencies that also have programs in the Ukraine.

For Terri and her husband, Jim, their decision to apply to a former state in the Soviet Union happened by chance. She said that her family was very supportive of their decision to adopt, whether domestically or internationally, though they were as concerned about the number of well-known "disruptions" found in domestic adoptions as were Terri and her husband. After attending adoption information meetings and reading as many books on the subject as they could get their hands on, the couple settled upon Russia:

> My husband was older at the time, meaning over forty-five, and quite honestly, we were not prepared to wait for years to have a family. We had a friend who knew of a lawyer who was working with an agency to help facilitate adoptions from Kazakhstan. I talked to him to get more information and he steered me towards an agency in Maine that was working in Russia as well. Not too long after meeting the lawyer, another friend told us about a couple they knew who had adopted successfully from Russia and encouraged us to call them. I did, and I don't know how to explain it, but I somehow knew we were supposed to go to Russia. We weren't really too concerned with matching our ethnicity since I am of Maltese and Irish descent and my husband is of Swedish and Irish descent.

One of the low points of Terri and Jim's experiences came soon after they had received their first assignments, a sibling group of three:

> We were interested in adopting a sibling group of preferably two kids. The director of the agency called me out of the blue to ask if we were willing to consider three kids, ages six, three, and eighteen months. Well, my gut instinct was 'why not?' Both my husband and I come from large families and we had always assumed we would have a house full of kids. You just never know how things will turn out. We were scheduled to travel to pick up the kids in July of '94, and were busily getting ready for our trip. We had even purchased our airplane tickets. About a week before our flight, we got a call from the agency telling us there was some sort of delay and that we would 'probably' travel in August. That didn't sound too reassuring, and I just kept thinking about those kids being in the orphan-

age even longer. Later, I was told it would be mid-September, though no real reason was given for the delay.

When the phone rang on September 9, Terri had a feeling it wasn't to report good news. It turned out she was right. The contact at their agency was calling to inform them that there had been some kind of a problem in getting the three children out of the country. The agency representative went on to say that she could not predict when, or even if, it would be possible.

Needless to say, that was pretty devastating news. She asked if we would consider going anyway but to take another sibling group from northern Russia. We talked for a long time and decided that this was God's will. We felt that we were supposed to let go of the three kids. It still saddens me, though, when I think about them and wonder if they've been adopted.

As Terri explained, they took a huge leap of faith and decided to leave for Russia on the eleventh as planned and meet their second assignments, Thomas, who turned five that day, and Mia, his younger brother, who was almost three.

After the emotional low of having to make a gut wrenching decision only two days earlier, it hardly seemed possible that we would be able to feel so happy a few days later. I know I cannot adequately describe the rush of emotion I felt when our kids walked into the room. We were all somewhat nervous and tentative, especially Thomas, since he had a better understanding of what was actually happening. Mia walked in and gave us the most incredible smile. I just couldn't do anything but smile back. We were in total awe. Only later, after we had left the orphanage to return to where we were staying for the night did it actually hit me: these are our kids! We felt so blessed.

The orphanage where the two children had been living was located in Apatity City, in the Murmansk region of northern Russia, adjacent to Finland. The sign on the door roughly translated into "House of Children." From the outside it resembled a two-story schoolhouse made of gray brick. Terri and Jim had no idea what to expect as they stood on the front steps. Once inside, they were pleasantly surprised with what they saw. The director and his wife appeared to be a loving couple, demonstratively devoted to the children. In terms of the physical surroundings, the walls were painted in bright, cheerful colors, many with murals; even the stairs were brightly painted.

The children were kept in groupings by age, each group sleeping in its own room. The rooms were furnished with twelve or fifteen little beds, all lined up with identical bedspreads and pillows. Every child had a locker for his or her belongings, although they didn't have many. Attached to each sleeping room was a play and learning area. Terri and Jim saw some of the children eating in another area with tables and chairs in groupings of four. Upon seeing the volume of developmental toys and books in the orphanage, Terri was, again, pleasantly surprised. Not only did they consider it clean and well maintained, but it seemed to be an institution full of warmth and caring. Her greatest fear was for the health of her kids. Would a major problem turn up later, one that they were not informed of? Any fear about bonding with her children was a relatively minor fear in comparison.

Jim's greatest fear, on the other hand, was precisely about bonding with their newly adopted children. "I think Jim was more concerned than I," she added, "especially after hearing some of the scary stories about children in institutions. I never felt like they rejected me in any way. Perhaps that was because the caregivers in the orphanage were all females," she reasoned.

> Both our boys were quite affectionate and always responsive to me. With my husband, the story was different. They were really unsure how to approach him. In fact, I think he was learning how to show affection to kids at the same time they were figuring out how to respond to it. Since returning home, we've discovered that both children display some behavior that is probably a function of their early life. They both seem to like order around them. They line things up (books, shoes, toys). They make their beds and are very independent in general. Mia was dressing himself at age three.

Uneasy Waiting

As adoptive parents, Harold and Kelly's experiences are relatively unique because, unlike the majority of parents you meet in these pages, they aren't married. They also had different views of adoption. Kelly initially started their foreign adoption proceedings. "At forty-one," Harold said, "her biological alarm clock went off." With time and understanding Kelly's decision to pursue a Russian adoption gradually became more acceptable to Harold, though he readily admits that he still has a preference for pursuing their own biological opportunities. Later, when several adoption assignments fell through, he turned to the internet for some answers and to share their experience.

On the basis of what Kelly perceives as the excessive rights of domestic birth parents to suddenly appear and snatch the kid years down the line, she settled upon Russia or Georgia, partially on the basis of deciding to adopt a kid who was of similar race, and partially on the basis of a pleasant summer she had spent in Russia doing amateur archaeology. The operating model here was that the adopted kids are to be hers, with her calling the shots. I can contribute as much as I want, but there is to be no clash of control. After proceeding with our home study, we signed on with an agency that handled Russian adoptions. Then things started getting weird. Last week's baby, with nothing but a name and birth date and travel on two-day's notice, fell through right away. This week Kelly got connected with another kid; plenty of info on this one, everything seemed OK. She talked with the Russian facilitators. It seemed really solid. Travel next Saturday, then another call: have to wait another month. She was receiving preliminary information on a bunch of kids, who turned out, in the end, not be be adoptable.

This isn't the way we pictured it. After extensive soul-searching and pouring out our wishes and dreams to the agency, which in exchange, promised that our referrals would be extensively screened and matched to our needs and desires by trained professionals, we end up, instead, feeling like we're standing in front of a fire hose that's squirting out babies and we're expected to grab one as it flies by.

Another person in the adoption field suggested switching agencies and recommended Children's Home Society of Minnesota, an agency that would not penalize clients if they declined the first, or even subsequent, referrals, and operated in a professional manner. He added, "My thoughts are that your agency is playing games with you. They should have all the information you need, and I can't imagine why they would withhold it from you."

At forty-five years of age, Harold spoke about his desire to attempt one more in vitro fertilization procedure while their biological opportunity still existed and revealed that funding both that and the adoption was an insurmountable problem. He is feeling less pessimistic, however, with each step forward in the adoption process. Harold continued to explain their situation:

> Not being married, I don't get included on Kelly's health care plan and vice versa. I also don't get time off for things like travel to Russia. So her mother will be going instead. I don't get paternity leave, either. It's definitely a separating factor. Yet, it seems wrong to get married just so I can share in the adoption bennies. Kelly had a year head start to get herself geared up for this. I have to catch up, though I seem to be more worried about getting a bad placement than she is. Most of the foreign adoptions we see here on the internet subscriber group have some medical problems, though nothing that can't be fixed.

MEMORIES OF ST. PETERSBURG

The experiences of these next two couples helps to clarify what waiting adoptive parents might expect when traveling to the Russian republics. Richard and his wife, Rosemary, traveling with two other couples, stayed in St. Petersburg at an Americanized apartment provided by their agency, Small World. The meals in Russia were very good, though Richard recommends not drinking the tap water. "Our cook, the drivers and interpreter provided us with bottled water.

Where they got it, I don't know," he added, "but it's probably a boom-
ing business over there." He stated that the worst part of the entire trip
was the nine-and-a-half hour return flight from Frankfurt to their
home town. "We didn't sleep," he said, "and neither did our son."
Other than that, things went very smoothly for all the couples who
traveled together to pick up their children.

> I'd say total time spent with the government officials there was
> three hours. All of them were pleasant to us and seemed gen-
> uinely happy for the children. The same goes for the Small
> World people: they were considerate, patient, concerned,
> empathetic, sympathetic and just plain nice people. We were
> treated as guests in their country and in return we treated them
> with respect and friendship.
>
> In St. Petersburg, we went to two different government
> offices, where we spent just enough time to sign some paper-
> work and get our son's birth and adoption certificates; the rest
> of the time was ours. Bring a camera and a compact video cam-
> era, because these will be memories to treasure forever. We will
> be using Small World again. They may be a tad more expensive
> than some other agencies, but I highly recommend them. That
> money goes to the kids at the orphanages.

Marsha and John, living in Missouri, were eager to tell their adoption story. Like Richard and Rosemary, their adopted son was also living in an orphanage in St. Petersburg. Marsha was thirty-eight at the
time of their only adoption, and her husband was fifty.

We met at a coffee shop and fell easily into conversation. Marsha
had mentioned a journal that she'd kept about her recent trip, as well
as on her feelings about adopting a child. She allowed me to read it
during our meeting. I found that gesture extremely moving—in part,
because journals are such personal things.

As I skimmed the hand-written pages, her feelings unfolded.

> As the adoption process continues, I'm feeling confused, dizzy
> and unable to concentrate. It's also very stimulating and excit-
> ing. I'm on pins and needles about the whole process. There
> seem to be obstacles and traps along the entire way, and you're

not sure when one is going to pop up. Sometimes, when a friend who is really concerned asks about how things are going, I can't talk about it. I'm scared.

She said, "We were told that the unadopted children are put out on the streets at fifteen or sixteen. Most resort to a life of crime or prostitution. Our greatest fear was that we would get a sick child and then the child would die." She feels that one advantage of adoption is the ability to request the age and sex of a child. The disadvantages are the unclear and often nonexistent medical information so common in international adoption.

Their son, Alexander, four years old at the time of his adoption, was raised in an orphanage in St. Petersburg. Marsha and John described it as being cool, musty smelling and dim. I asked her what advice she might pass along to other prospective adoptive parents. Her response, "What can go wrong will, so be prepared! Unfortunately, the laws and the governments are very discouraging for adoptive couples. They put you through hell." The journal continued to include life with their son at home in Missouri. I asked Marsha if she and her husband noticed any behavior that was indicative of their son's orphanage upbringing? I hoped to dispel some of the commonly heard horror stories about orphanages from around the world—stories of children being tied to their cribs, starving or eventually dying.

Everyday he's learning new English. I love to hear him sing songs in Russian. He hasn't learned to play in his room yet. I suppose I need to teach him that it's not only a place to sleep, (spatz,) but also a place to have fun. As for behavior related to the orphanage—Alexander tears off a tiny piece of a Kleenex when he uses one, instead of using the whole tissue. I suppose supplies were short in the orphanage, and the children learned to make do with what they had.

A Little Girl from Kirov and A Dying Mother-In-Law

It was an orphanage in Kirov that brought a six-month-old daughter into the arms of Leonard and Julia, two people that come from stable families, have MBAs and are homebodies who enjoy gardening and cooking. Julia is thirty-seven and a career woman. Though the couple's decision to adopt was a very natural one, almost a self-fulfilling prophecy, Julia never thought she could get so attached to any child as she has to their adopted daughter, Anna. "I always knew I'd adopt a child in my life," Julia began, "and Leonard desperately wanted a family. We just had to decide when to start planning one." They had been married for four years when Julia became pregnant, then suffered a miscarriage. After four more years without another pregnancy, Leonard and Julia decided they had been on the infertility roller coaster long enough. "Every other day I started with a run to the lab," Julia explained, "then an intrusive exam at the doctor's office, and finally an injection of drugs at night." Because of the level of drugs she was taking, Julia maintained this schedule for only two weeks. It was a hard two weeks, for she had to juggle her demanding high-profile corporate job and try to realize their goal of having a family simultaneously. Quitting her job to focus solely on getting pregnant would have created an unhealthy emotional situation. "Besides," Julia added, "the dual income and insurance coverage helped cover part of our fertility treatments." She detailed her sentiments on the role financial considerations play in an adoption.

It is unfortunate, but a reality, that your financial situation is an essential cog in the decision-making process. If you decide to spend your bank account on fertility treatments in order to have a biological child and you fail, you no longer have the finances to pursue an adoption. At the beginning, we both decided to continue treatments up to the maximum allowance available through our plan. In this way, our out-of-pocket expenses would be kept to a minimum and we would not get caught in the Catch 22 trap, 'let's try it one more time.' It's all too tempting to get back into treatment after an emotionally devastating failure. Deciding up front on when to quit turned out to be the best decision of our lives.

The couple's decision to adopt enabled Julia to regain control over her life and her body. She was not the type of person to take even an aspirin for a headache, much less the many powerful drugs she'd been injecting. After contacting some agencies that sent literature on specific countries, they selected Russia. "Leonard didn't want the child to wear a sign saying, 'I'm adopted,' and since both of our maternal grandmothers came from Russia, it seemed like a natural place to start."

Next, the couple talked about what age child they would adopt. Julia was surprised to learn that her husband wanted an infant, while she wanted to adopt an older child. At thirty-seven, Leonard said he wanted to experience everything, and the couple compromised: they requested a child one year of age or under. She also was surprised by his gender request.

Next came the sex preference question on our application. I said, 'Don't even bother. I prefer a boy. You know, carry on your name.' Well, again Leonard surprised me by saying that he didn't want to specify a sex. Totally stunned, I asked, 'Why not?' He said he didn't want to play God and whatever child was meant to be our child would be our child. It amazed me that he came to the adoption decision with definite adoption thoughts. He wholeheartedly accepted this child, and I knew how much he wanted a biological child. I was so proud of him.

After four changes in their travel plans, the couple's eventual trip to Russia became a race against time. Leonard's mother was dying. The day after Christmas she was admitted to the hospital with advanced cancer. Leonard and Julia were in complete shock. "How could we let ourselves enjoy the coming of the newest member of the family while facing the biggest loss of our young lives?" asked Julia. With each travel cancellation, the tension mounted. His mother wanted to see her first grandchild more than she wanted a vigil. The couple was tormented with the inevitable: "Do we postpone, or do we go?" Leonard shared with his mother the one picture they had of their daughter, Anna. They decided to go ahead as planned. Upon return, the first day of February, they brought their newly adopted daughter to visit her grandmother. Four days later, Leonard's mother died.

While at the Kirov orphanage, they were told the name and age of Anna's biological mother, the name of her father, and the reason they cited for giving the baby up. They were told the parents were not married and that Anna was not her biological mother's first pregnancy. But there was no medical background or religious information on the parents. Julia and her husband plan on giving their daughter what little information they have, but admit that it will probably be impossible for Anna to track down her biological parents. When the couple was in Russia, Julia asked the host if a mother ever asks or checks back with the orphanage to see if her baby got adopted. "She shook her head and said that I was thinking like an American. Once the baby is relinquished, the mother gets on with her life. No one in her family showed any interest in Anna." Julia revealed what having their daughter means to her and what plans the couple has for Anna as their life together develops:

Anna is my life, the center of my universe. She keeps me focused. I've cut back on my work hours, take time off during the week to spend with her, get down on the floor and play, and give her lots of cuddles and kisses. When she curls up in my arms to fall asleep, I just shake my head and realize how much time I lost. But, I wasn't ready to be a mother. I wanted time for me and time alone with my husband. We wanted to take a real honeymoon. Anna is our reward.

Leonard and I are both Jewish, but not religious. We plan on teaching Anna a little about each major Jewish holiday. Her Russian culture is also important. My niece goes to classes to learn Hebrew, to learn the holidays and to interact with other Jewish children. This is not for us. We'd prefer it if Anna learned more about Russia, its language, culture and traditions. Together with our holiday traditions, we hope she will not feel like we've abandoned her background, but blended it into our family.

She described their daughter's behavior at six months of age as calm and friendly, and noted that their adjustment period was very easy. "She was holding her head up, pulling to a standing position and bouncing. She would let anyone hold her. She didn't cry, not for a bottle, for food or for bedtime. I thought this very curious." Finally, Julia said that she never tires of explaining how Anna entered their lives.

What I find interesting is that when strangers interact with her and remark how well behaved she is, or what a healthy appetite she has, or how special she seems, I find I tell them her story. They usually tell their own story of someone they know who has plans to adopt. It reaffirms our appreciation for having her touch our lives. Right now, Anna is too young to understand these conversations. When she's older, I'll curb my conversations with strangers, as it will become her business who she wants to tell. I think she'll enjoy meeting other adopting couples and their children as much as Leonard and I do.

My husband and I have already agreed that when she gets older, it would be nice to instill a sense of compassion and generosity for someone less fortunate than she. If, and when, she has large birthday parties, I'll ask her to donate one of her many toys to charity. No child absolutely needs or has the time to play with thirty new toys, a few of them duplicates. I hope Anna will understand where she came from and that she now has the opportunity, even at a young age, to help others.

QUESTIONS AND ANSWERS

Of the thousands of parents who are still waiting to adopt their Russian children, or merely contemplating the idea of such an adoption, many are searching for answers and for emotional support unavailable through more conventional means. They have very specific questions about agencies, orphanages, medical histories, legal and administrative procedures, and care of the children, and they are looking for specific answers:

~ Does anybody have any recommendations for agencies in the Washington D. C. area?

~ I am traveling to Rostov-on-Don to pick up our child. He is at Maya's Baby Home. Does anyone know of this home?

~ I have heard that the babies are fed cow's milk. Can anyone confirm this? If so, did anyone have trouble transitioning from cow's milk to formula?

~ Is it easy to find diapers and formula in Russia?

~ Has anyone adopted a child with a speech delay? How significant have speech delays been for other parents?

~ What is "disarticulation"?

~ Can I call an "800" number from Russia? If so, any idea of the cost?

~ We've received a list from our agency of gifts and other items to take with us, but does anyone have any more suggestions?

~ We received a video of a little boy and a one-page information sheet. Shouldn't we have received a medical statement as well?

~ My understanding is that the children in Russia have been tested for Hepatitis B and that it should not be a concern, but I still wonder. Can a person rely on such tests?

Oftentimes, again, the speed of the internet makes that the easiest route to a much needed answer. Calling agencies for a quick response can result in frustration for the preadoptive parents. In many cases, individuals who have already adopted are making helpful contributions on-line. For example, two separate commentaries were offered in reply to the question about children with speech delays. "Regarding speech delay: it depends upon how old the child is. My oldest, whom I adopted after his fourth birthday, was speech delayed. He had a very limited Russian vocabulary and communicated more with gestures than words." Another person wrote, "We were told that our kids, ages four, six, and seven, had speech delays prior to leaving Russia. By this, the doctor meant that their language was not so developed as you would expect for children their ages. At the time, this was not a worrisome concern. Both kids have since become fully fluent in English without any special tutoring."

In response to the question about the reliability of testing for Hepatitis B, one person replied, "Absolutely *do not* rely on the results of any tests done in Russia, or immunizations either, for that matter. Have all tests and immunizations done at home. I would suggest you test for HIV, Hepatitis B, and sickle cell and for intestinal parasites like Giardia."

The following is typical of the concerns about selecting a qualified, reputable adoption agency.

My husband thinks I must have requested information from every agency on the planet because of the daily packages that arrive in the mail. Although I enjoy reading and learning about all the different programs, sometimes they seem a little 'too good to be true.' And the fees are all outlined so differently. Some list exactly what services are included, others are pretty generic. What are the important services to look for when selecting an agency?

Among the responses about criteria for selecting an agency, an anonymous individual replied, "Ask the agency how many orphanages they currently work with and in how many regions. Ask the agency, when it's working in several different regions, if it will still be receiving referrals from other areas if one of them slows down? Ask about the age ranges of the children who come from each of the orphanages. The answers to these questions should help determine what the chances are of getting an infant, toddler, or older child." One couple recommended World Child Agency and had a very positive experience to report. Another individual used Adoptions Together, Inc. in Baltimore and described them as being a very caring and honest agency. Finally, another internet user forwarded the web site address for the Consular Affairs Department of the Department of State in Washington, D. C., which has information on international adoptions.[1]

For clarification on some of the other concerns and issues, I contacted the director of Global Adoption Service, Inc. in Moscow after reading several of his informative posts on the internet. I asked him if he'd share some of the most frequent inquiries he receives from people considering adoption, or at the beginning stages of the process. Here is his reply:

Q. If homeland Russians have first choice of children, does that minimize the number of healthy infants for international adoption?

A. Not really, because the number of families in the Russian population who are willing to adopt is lower than the number of children coming available for adoption. Russian families are small, usually no more than two children, yet modern birth control methods are not readily available. Thus, there are a larger number of children available for adoption per capita than in most western countries. The result is more available healthy children than most other countries of similar racial and cultural background.

Q. How prevalent is Fetal Alcohol Syndrome?

A. It does exist. But my opinion is that it is no more prevalent in Russia than for orphaned children in most other countries. The same problem exists in the United States, plus there's the added problem for a child of a mother's drug addiction.

Q. What is the time period from submitting our paperwork to referral, then from referral to travel?

A. From submitting paperwork to referral, it depends on the region. For most regions, maybe six to eight months for kids under one year— shorter for older children, almost immediate for special needs children. From referral to travel, it depends again upon the region. For most regions, maybe one or two months; it takes a little time to get all the paperwork prepared for your arrival, and for you to prepare to come.

Q. My agency is supposedly one of the most reputable adoption agencies in the United States but I'm losing my patience with them and my trust in them as well. Do you know anything about any problems in Russia? Would you have any other ideas as to what is causing the delay?

A. Well, I can understand your frustration. We estimate that at least 2,500 foreign requests for children in the Moscow region are sitting on the desks of Moscow officials right now. And the parents all want these requests to be filled this month—in fact, immediately! Young baby girls are at a premium right now. It seems that at least 80 percent of the parents in my agency make that their first request. So statistically, that means that about two thousand new baby girls would have to be given to the orphanages this month for all the requests to be filled. That just isn't going to happen.

I hope that you can understand the frustration of your adoption coordinators when so many of their clients want the same thing. They are doing their best to fill every request in a personal, understanding way. If you were working with my agency, I would be telling you something very similar to what you are hearing from yours—please be patient, your time will come before too long. I know that sounds hollow after almost a year of waiting already. Perhaps the only real comfort is to know that you are not alone.

My wife, Yelena, keeps reminding me that it took a Russian mother (and every other) nine months to actually carry her baby to term, and then go through a very painful experience to give the child birth, and then to give it up. Sometimes it seems that the Russians are trying to make you go through a similar process to adopt the child. As I said before in this forum, maybe the universe is teaching us something about the value of human commitment, devotion and real love. I've come to believe that.

Q. How long does it take to adopt an infant girl?

A. First of all, I'd like to invite you to work with us. But we are by no means the only agency capable of helping you. Just yesterday I saw a couple with a beautiful infant girl from Siberia—found through an agency I had never heard of before. It's being done by well-known agencies and by the quiet and inconspicuous ones. We have a history of placing both healthy infant girls and boys. About one-third of our placements are in that category; one-sixth are healthy girls under two years old. We have identified, and are now placing, twin infant girls, three months old, blonde hair, blue eyes. The parents are traveling the end of June. Three days ago we were promised five infant girls from a region in the Ural mountains. Yes, we have parents waiting for those children, but none have been waiting over nine months. We are now opening a new region in Siberia that's very exciting, because very few agencies have been allowed to work there.

Q. My wife and I are about three weeks away from our second trip to Moscow to pick up our son. Could you please e-mail us and let us know what the procedure will be when we get there?

A. My answer depends upon whether you are picking up your child in Moscow itself or in one of the regions. In Moscow, you will follow a procedure something like this:

- Arrive at Moscow Sherimetravo II Airport.
- Look out your airplane window and wonder why hundreds of empty airplanes are parked on the runway.
- Go through passport check, one at a time.
- Rent a damaged baggage cart for 10,000 rubles, or $2.00.
- Wonder how the ruble could be worth so little, and what that did to old grandmother's life savings.
- Wonder if you will lose your life savings.
- As you leave customs, find your coordinator waiting patiently, holding your name on a large cardboard box cover.
- Outside the airport doors, fill a small car with too much luggage.
- Marvel at all the dirt and dust—on everything.
- Ride into Moscow and enjoy the chaos.
- Meet your host family at their apartment or check into the hotel.
- Try out your Russian.
- Meet your adoption coordinator and discuss details of the day.
- Go to orphanage and pick up your child!
- Hold your child. Forget about everything else!
- Give gifts to the orphanage director.
- Complete a short thirty-minute exam of the child for INS, then file and sign forms.
- Visit the passport photo shop next to the American Embassy.
- Wait in an extremely cramped room with twenty other couples and their children until your name is called for your visa appointment.
- Meet the embassy worker in charge of your case. Talk through a very thick glass window. Wonder if the worker was once a bank teller.
- Review everything again.
- Visit the largest MacDonald's in the world on Arbat Street.
- Come back at exactly 5 P.M. that day and pick up the child's visa!
- Sleep a wonderful night with your new child near you.
- Rise and pack, with a lot less than you brought.
- Be taken to the airport.
- Show off your new child to anyone who will give you attention.
- Watch Moscow disappear, as you rise into the clouds with your new family.

POLICIES CAN CHANGE FASTER THAN THE WEATHER

Like any adventurous activity, adoption can generate its own rumors. Changes in governmental policies lead to many of them. A representative example from the internet illustrates the point: "Just heard that there are new rules in Russia: no more than four kids from each region can be adopted monthly. Anyone hear about that?"

The internet is a great way for agencies, including Global Adoption Services, to spread the word about themselves. It's also a valuable tool to let subscribers to a growing list of adoption newsgroups know about updated policy changes. Often, however, it's personal experience that speaks the loudest. This update from the Moscow director of Global Adoption Services is typical of the Russian adoption process at the time.

We just got a letter from the Counselor of the Embassy at Consular Affairs, which makes it clear that the American Embassy will no longer accept the Form I-171 for the purpose of proving the approval of your "Application for Advance Processing of Orphan Petition" (I-600A) by the Immigration and Naturalization Service (INS). Only a telegram or a facsimile of the actual approved form I-600A itself will do. May 6 is the last day they will accept the I-171 H form. Due to the number of cases being handled, the embassy staff asks that you "Please do not contact us by facsimile or by telephone from the United States to confirm that we have received INS approval. If you have received your "Dear Parents" letter, you may assume that the Embassy has received cabled notification from the INS.

When we, your Russian agents, call or go into the embassy to make an appointment for your visa interview, we will be able to ask and get confirmation that they have received notice of INS approval. If they have not received anything from the INS, you, the adopting parents, need to call the INS office that approved your I-600A to get that notification sent to the embassy by fax.

Remember—the family who arrives for the visa interview after May 5 without the appropriate INS notification will be advised to contact their INS office to request that the embassy be sent the required fax. One of the major changes resulting from implementing regulations for the adoption law passed in March '95 is that both parents are required to travel to Russia to receive the adoption certificate and take custody of the child. Some local authorities, however, are not applying every aspect of the law in a uniform manner. Whether to risk attempting to complete the adoption process with something less than what the law requires, or not is a decision for the prospective adoptive parents. Your agency may tell you one thing, but you may arrive to find that the local authority has changed its mind.

In the event that only one parent travels, he or she must present, at the time of the immigrant visa interview, a completed Form I-600 petition on which the absent parent's signature has been notarized by a notary public. Note: the power of attorney that the traveling spouse might carry will not allow him or her to sign the Form I-600 petition in lieu of his or her absent spouse—irrespective of what the language on the power of attorney says!

Finally, let me wish you all good luck!

---

[1] Web site address for the Bureau of Consular Affairs Department: http://travel.state.gov or write for the general information pamphlet, Consular Affairs, CA/P/PA, Room 6831, U. S. Department of State, Washington, DC 20520-4818

CHAPTER 6

From Many Lands

If we are to achieve a richer culture, rich in contrasting values, we must recognize the whole gamut of human potentialities, and so we are a less arbitrary social fabric, one in which each diverse human gift will find a fitting place.

—Margaret Mead from *Sex and Temperament* copyright 1935, 1950, 1963. By permission of HarperCollins Publishers, Inc.

THOUGH THE LARGEST NUMBER OF ADOPTED CHILDREN WHO ENTERED THE United States in 1996 were from Korea,[1] many other countries also permit adoptions—countries like Bolivia, Mexico, Costa Rica, Nicaragua and Romania to name a few. For Jackie and her husband, two children, one from a South American country, Peru, and one from a Central American country, Guatemala, changed their lives forever.

Jackie's first desire was to have a biological child. Her medical history is an example of what can dash such hopes. She had bad tubes, endometriosis, lupus, and trouble ovulating, and she needed hormonal assistance. If that wasn't discouraging enough, she lost four pregnancies, including one set of twins in an ectopic pregnancy. She had attempted pregnancy for thirteen years, through two marriages and two doctors. "I would wear a black garter belt on my leg and make the doctor and nurses laugh," she said. Her sense of humor helped her to endure. The common thread during this span of time was disappointment. She endured so many operations, that her belly button, which had been an "outie," became an "innie."

After every miscarriage, Jackie called adoption agencies, but was discouraged by the price and the length of time the process would take. She felt it was cheaper to try again to get pregnant. At that time, she considered adoption a second choice. When she and her husband, Hugh, eventually did decide upon adoption, however, they proceeded in earnest to complete the necessary paperwork. Today, she thinks adoption is the best way to build a family.

The first child assigned to them was born in Peru, a darling three-and-a-half-month-old girl they named Meagan Molly. It was November of 1991 then, and both parents-to-be were thirty-five. They traveled with eleven other couples. Their planned two-week trip, however, turned into a much longer stay. Thanksgiving, Christmas, and New Year holidays were spent in what Jackie termed, "an often frightening foreign country."

Twelve weeks after their departure, they returned with their daughter. "The holidays were the worst," she continued, "but my daughter and I bonded so well during those months that I feel she was truly my birth child who was 'put' in another woman's body for nine months. We are still very close." On four different occasions Jackie and Hugh were able to meet their daughter's birth parents, meetings many adopting singles and couples desire. Jackie described them as being wonderful young people, eighteen years of age. "We gave them food, pots, dishes, toys, and household items all wrapped up as Christmas gifts." She added, "We were nervous about meeting them, but it was the best! We still write letters and send pictures twice a year. I want them to be content that they did the right thing."

For their second adoption, the couple traveled to Guatemala to pick up the son they would name David. He was nine months old. Guatemala seems to present everything other Central American countries have to offer in a condensed and exaggerated form: its volcanoes are the highest and most active, its Mayan ruins the most impressive, its population the largest, and its earthquakes some of the most devastating. Agency documents shared with adoptive parents prior to their travel typically mention the country's conditions, and warn parents traveling there to avoid excursions after dark and to keep their valuables out of sight. Guatemala has had enough hostile incidents to prompt their legislature to pass a recent bill promising the death sentence for anyone caught kidnapping a foreigner.

A trip into a foreign country can be, and often is, quite unnerving. This trip was no exception. Jackie remembered waiting for the lawyers to arrive the first day at their hotel in Guatemala to make the final legal arrangements; they arrived almost three hours late. During the wait, Jackie, David, and Hugh ventured outside to take a picture of the hotel. Suddenly, ten policemen came up and questioned them on why they had with them a child who was obviously of a different ethnic origin.

We showed them what little documentation we had with us. Meanwhile, crowds formed. It was embarrassing. Their interrogation lasted four grueling hours. David was crying. I tried to be calm, look innocent, smile, avoid looking at their guns and not burst into tears. Forget the money, or the paper work or the agency stringing us along. We had to wait and pray forever to finally get our children into our lives. They mean more to us than words can express. We went across the world to get them. I've been called a hero, but I feel like I was a very desperate person. I was willing to do anything to become a mother. That's why we're in the middle of adoption number three—in the Philippines. All they have there are earthquakes and volcanoes! (And they'll probably hit when we're there!)

KOREA OFFERS ANSWERS

For another couple, Frank and Frances of West Virginia, their lifetime dream was realized by a child from South Korea, a country whose religions include Christianity, Buddhism, Confucianism, Shamanism and Chondogyo, the religion of the Heavenly Way. It took a major disappointment before they were able to share the joyous experience of holding their Korean-born son. Over the course of a year and a half they experienced the ups and downs of preparing for an adoption and had looked at several options, "including an unhealthy dose of denial."

Through their long preparation, they bared their souls, asked numerous people numerous questions, and were on the receiving end of many other questions. It's a story, unfortunately, that includes the death of a little girl who was lost to Sudden Infant Death Syndrome (SIDS).

Frank began their story:

Finally, the day arrived that we were to drive to Washington, D.C., to look at a picture of our assignment. Our expectations had peaked. On the way over, my wife was in tears. We were on our way to see the baby of our future. Was there any doubt we would accept it? We were trying off and on for over eight years to have a biological child. The night before, we collected small memorabilia, making a note that described our hopes for this child, to know that it was loved from the moment we knew of it. We couldn't sleep, our level of anticipation was too high. Frances cried immediately with big tears of joy as soon as we got the news. As the strong masculine type, I smiled, got misty-eyed and thought she was a real sweetie. We accepted her and could almost feel her in our arms. Within a few weeks, my wife revisited her family. Her sisters piled infant clothes and toys into our truck and we held our breaths all the way home. We couldn't get over how our announcement of bringing a child into our lives affected so many of our friends and family members.

A few days later, I was interrupted at a business meeting. I feared there was bad news. My father-in-law had just gone through open heart surgery and was at the critical stage of observation. When I met Frances she was in tears. I thought that her father must have passed away. What I wasn't expecting was the real news: we had lost our little girl in Korea to SIDS. The strong masculine side cracked and fell like dust to the floor. My life felt shattered. It was as though this little girl whom we hadn't even seen yet had so enmeshed her life with ours that her passing was as though she had been taken from my very arms. There was no way to fight it.

Frank recalled immediately seeking out a favorite park where they could walk and talk about what had happened. It was a cold afternoon, so they decided to get a hot cup of tea at a restaurant in the park, where they ran into some of Frances' fellow employees. One of them had already heard of the couple's sad news by way of a beeper. Suddenly, they were surrounded by friends. Frank mentioned how the entire group cried together. Everyone was touched by what had happened to their daughter, whom they had already named Mary Jo. They realized through their sorrow how strongly an intangible presence can seep into and hold onto a person's soul. They also became determined not to give up.

By the time they reached home, a note from the local social worker was on their door: "Tried to reach you, will call as soon as I can." Within minutes, their pastor arrived. Within an hour, the first flowers arrived. Before evening came, the first food basket arrived. Expressions of sympathy and support came from friends and family. Frank acknowledged that these gestures of caring brought home the knowledge that Mary Jo was truly dead. With each arrival of flowers, it was one more acknowledgment that forced the couple to face the little baby's passing:

> We received friends, prayers, cards, flowers and food for several days. Mary Jo had passed away in Korea on a Thursday, we knew that on Friday. It was good to mourn for a full three days. The pain of Mary Jo's loss has dulled, but it will never completely fade. We still have our momentos, which were to be the beginning of an identity scrapbook for her. Such things are not easy to part with. The following Monday, however, I called the D.C. agency and requested that we be considered for another child as soon as possible. I did this through tears, because the loss of our daughter was too fresh. Our representative wanted us to talk with the social worker at the agency before we truly made such a commitment.

Within three months, Frank and Frances were given the news that another picture awaited them, a picture of their son, Mark. Did they do anything differently when they heard about Mark?

> Yes. We were more hesitant about sharing the news with friends and family. If you're waiting in the adoption process or are contemplating adoption, our advice to you is 'full steam

ahead.' Don't hesitate, don't grow anxious, don't grow cautious. Instead, bathe in the joy of expectation, the celebration of life and the happiness of knowing that a bundle of joy awaits you. My dream was to see my wife dressing our little girl in a beautiful white dress for an Easter Sunday service. That dream hasn't changed; I still see our little girl. The new dream I have is of myself and our little boy standing quietly holding hands as the sun sets, and he asks, 'Daddy, why can't the sun stay where it is, it's so bright and beautiful right now.'

South Korea, which set up one of the first international programs established in the 1980s, also brought a child to another couple from halfway around the world. Rachel and Donald said that the entire subject brings up feelings both of great sadness and of great joy. From the first day of their infertility struggle, Rachel knew they would ultimately have a family, either with the help of technology or through adoption. When others in her infertility support group talked about lives without children, she thought such an option was incomprehensible.

Rachel feels that men generally have a harder time embracing the concept of adoption, due perhaps to the "passing along the genes to a son" issue. She supported her thought, "Our social worker said that a few years ago a study on adoption revealed that 80 percent of the parents specified wanting a girl for their first child. The high number was attributed to the fact that a girl usually doesn't carry on the family name after marriage, so it doesn't matter if she isn't genetically related. In our case, my husband was just the opposite."

The couple had considered several names—Timothy, Bradley and Adam—before finally settling on Alec. They wanted a name that wasn't likely to be carried by two or three others in their son's class. "We were always in agreement about the middle name being Mark," said Rachel, "and I also thought it was important to include part of his Korean name as a second middle name. Don didn't want to use the Korean name at first," she continued, "but I found several articles that indicated that some adoptees appreciated that link to their heritage, so he agreed. I wish, though, that his biological mother would have named him instead of the Korean social worker."

The first time they saw their son's picture was in July 1995. Rachel described their son as having a lot of dark hair and chubby cheeks. "He seemed so tiny sitting in his foster mom's lap. I don't think I fell in love the moment I saw his picture, but did so gradually as I looked at it every day." Seeing this picture meant there was light at the end of the tunnel. Three months later, she held her son for the first time. Rachel had thought she would be an emotional basket case; surprisingly, it was her husband who cried.

> I remember not being able to eat anything except a few crackers that day, and being worried about Alec adjusting to United States time. A Korean escort flew him to Los Angeles, and we met them at the airport and then flew home. The four-hour flight home was when I started bonding with him, but I think it took two or three months for the bonding to be complete.

Soon after settling in, the couple sent out special announcements to family and friends. Unable to decide which message they liked the best, they decided to mail out two announcements, one to family and another one to friends. On the cover of the announcement that was sent to family members was a picture of a Korean baby boy, on the inside the following:

> We search for our reflection
> In our precious children's eyes.
> We hope to see the remnants
> That heredity supplies.
>
> And though we'll never hear it said
> Our looks are much the same
> This special little child is ours,
> And bears our family name...
>
> — author unknown

Throughout the process, until they actually got Alec, Donald kept his emotional distance. "I tried to back off from talking about the adoption every single minute, which was very hard," Rachel explained. What continued to surprise her was her husband's changed attitude, once Alec became part of their family. "Alec has started saying, 'Da -Da,' and when he does, Donald just beams. He has taken to being a father much better than I thought he would. At times, I thought he was going through with the adoption just to please me, but I know now that it's not the case."

The thing she enjoys most about parenting is feeding their son his bottle while rocking him to sleep. "My arms ached so long to hold my child, so now that he's home," she said, "I hold him for a few extra minutes every day and appreciate it while he's so small. It's amazing how something so simple can mean so much."

The most frustrating element of their experience was dealing with the INS, a sentiment mirrored by other adoptive individuals. When she and her husband delivered the I-600 form and other legal documents in person to the government office, they were told the approval would be cabled to South Korea the next day. Two weeks later, after several letters written to the Senators of Texas complaining about the delay, a cable was sent. "Now it almost seems kind of silly that we got so angry over two weeks," she added, "but back then it was a lifetime."

To Linda and Al, a military couple, Korean culture has been part of their lives since Al was first stationed in South Korea. The expanded family now lives in Oregon with their two children—their first child, who was biological, and their second, a Korean girl. "Names have great meaning in Korea and are chosen carefully," explained Linda. "Our daughter's name at birth was Mee Ok, which means, 'beautiful jewel.'" They picked up their daughter when she was six weeks old and living with a family in Seoul. Linda continued:

My greatest fear during the time that we were waiting for the adoption to be finalized was that we would loose Mee Ok. We had originally stated in filing our papers that I couldn't get pregnant, but, to our surprise, I was able to conceive later. My second fear was that South Korea would go to war and I would be sent home to the states. We were told that if this were to happen, our daughter would not be allowed to leave the country with me. Finalized adoption was the key, in this instance because our daughter wasn't legally ours at this point and could not leave her country. This fear was brought on by the three alerts that we were put on. I cried and hugged my daughters the minute we stepped onto American soil in Oregon. I'm sure everyone on the plane thought I was loony, but I didn't care, I was home.

To another woman, raising two adopted children from South Korea has become incredibly more difficult with the recent death of her husband. "I feel so horrible. Thank God I have my two beautiful children...they are the only things keeping me going right now," she began. "I'm grateful that this didn't happen abroad." Tina recalled she and her husband's experience with infertility, including one physician's recommendation that Tina loose twenty five pounds.

In addition to being told I should lose some weight, another doctor said that I was too focused on becoming pregnant. Nevertheless, we were inseminated (what a wonderful experience that was) many times. At one point, after my sixth insemination, I remember lying on the exam table, crying, then looking up at my husband and saying, 'No more.' I felt like cattle being bred. That was the last time I went to an infertility doctor to try to conceive. From then on, Jeff and I went about our lives together. Our new focus was on each other only...working and taking vacations and 'enjoying' our lives, while publicly avoiding the subject of children. There was a period when we took a job as 'house-parents' for mentally retarded youths who were de-institutionalized. In hindsight, I think living with these boys for two years fulfilled my need to be 'somebody's mother.' Eventually, though, that wasn't enough.

They had been married seven years when her husband initially brought up the subject of adoption. At first, they considered local or private adoption, but soon were given a rude wake-up call. Although they were willing to take a biracial or Hispanic baby (they're Caucasian), the agency told them they wouldn't place one with them, feeling that they couldn't offer such children the heritage they needed for proper identity. "How I cried! Didn't they know that I would be a great mother?" she asked. Still resentful of this decision, Tina thinks it's most important for a child to be unconditionally loved. Self-identity and self-esteem, she believes, are created by what type of life a person leads early on and what tools a person is given from the outset to deal with all of life's pressures.

Racial issues didn't cause them any concern, although one grandparent professed to be a bigoted man. At first, he said that if this was what they wanted, he would try and accept the children, but not to expect him to love them the same as his other grandchildren. They were steered toward international adoptions because of their fear of the domestic process. They eventually met, and became friends with, a couple who adopted an Asian baby and steered them to the agency they had used. After adopting, the couple was warned about outsiders' reactions to their mixed family. Early on, the children were coached not to respond to rude questions. "Strangers used to see us and ask us if the children were ours and if we knew about their backgrounds? I asked them why they needed to know such personal things about a stranger. I would never think to ask some of the things I've been asked." Then she explained the toughest aspect of adopting:

The most difficult part was two-fold. First is the waiting, which, can be dreadful. With the first child we adopted, our son, now eleven, the wait was a tolerable ten months from the time our paperwork arrived in South Korea until he arrived in New York. Claudia, our daughter, now seven, took longer. Since we were taking medical risks with her, it took time to correspond back and forth with questions and answers. With her, it took fourteen months. The second difficult part was the correspondence regarding medical information...very frustrating.

INDIA IS THEIR ANSWER

India is a huge country, a subcontinent actually, with perhaps as much diversity as Europe. Its people speak a wide variety of languages, and the climate runs to extremes—from the Great Indian Desert in the northwest to the humid tropics of the south, to the mountains of the northeast. In terms of social class, you'll find small village farmers to urban poor living in shanties to the upper classes, whose lives more closely resemble the lives of people living in the Western industrialized nations. If you're planning a trip for an adoption and are in control of your travel time, travel agents generally recommend traveling during the spring or fall, to avoid the premonsoon and monsoon months. If you do have to travel in the summer, they warn, beware—it's not the heat alone that is stifling, but the dust together with the hot winds.

Some couples, like Chloe and her husband, Jack, easily accepted the Indian culture and decided to look there for their international adoption. They adopted nine years ago, when Chloe was forty, after having two biological children, and after thirteen years of marriage. She admits to being too selfish for many years to consider parenting. "I needed to parent myself for a long time. I was adopted, and it was not a happy experience."

The couple settled upon India for several reasons: first, they had friends who had adopted Indian children; next, because India's adoption program was open to them; and finally, because they felt that they could honestly help a child keep its culture while living here in America.

Initially, it was her husband who wanted more children, but Chloe didn't have the drive to have another child. The couple didn't consider domestic adoption because they didn't meet the requirements for adopting an infant, and because they didn't want the attachment problems sometimes associated with adopting an older child.

Since the adoption of their daughter, Jill, they have experienced both the joys and obstacles that parenting a language-impaired child brings. Chloe has learned some rather unpleasant things about herself through the process, negative things. In dealing with their daughter's problem, Chloe has also learned, though, that she has more patience than she thought she had.

Getting a child who is language impaired has changed all of us. We are very verbal and have had to adjust to what Jill can do. It has been, and is, very difficult. We are very different emotionally. Jill is easily upset because she can't always follow what is going on. I hate being screamed at. So I'm learning not to yell back, sort of. And when she's upset, talking to her is even harder, so I keep having to learn new approaches. I'm a writer and a teacher and fairly quiet by nature. So this is a challenge. Adopting our daughter certainly strengthened my faith in God, once I got over being furious with Him for sending us a child with problems when all I asked for was a normal kid. It's now much easier for me to trust in God to show me the correct solution.

Having lived in India as a Rotary International Exchange Student in '73 and '74, another mother, Carol, was already familiar with the country when it was time for her and her husband, Chris, to consider adopting. They ended up adopting three children, all high-risk premature infants, abandoned at birth. The first child was four months old at adoption, the second thirteen months, and the last six months. When they decided to adopt, Carol's familiarity with India was an important factor but they also preferred international adoption because of their distaste for what Carol termed the "white baby sweepstakes." They chose to go with International Mission of Hope (IMH) in Calcutta, West Bengal. They did their home study locally, and then applied to IMH through Families of Children of Various Nations (FCVN) in Denver. They were accepted in February of '87 and received a referral of a baby boy four months later.

By early September the boy's visa was issued, and they were, as Chris termed it, awaiting the "stork call." Instead, they received a cable telling them that their agency suspected cerebral palsy—one health problem they felt unequipped to handle. They let him go. Two weeks later, they got another referral; six weeks later had their son, Leo, in their arms. Integrating two cultures into everyday life can be challenging, Carol explained. "It's difficult to build Indian customs into our everyday lives," she said. Then I asked Carol if she felt there were some misconceptions about international adoption.

> The international adoption community is a self-selected group, different from the 'healthy Caucasian infant' community in many ways. There seems to be a pretty good understanding about the realities of international adoption among this group. Recently, the international community has had its ranks bolstered by a number of people attracted by the opening-up of eastern Europe (white children available!). This group has often worked with agencies with less background in international adoption and has not always been well-screened and taught. Consequently, many people went into their adoption thinking that somehow institutionalized white children were OK to adopt, while they would never have considered institutionalized nonwhite children. There have been a lot of heartaches and quite a number of disruptions because of this kind of 'magical' thinking.

Experts know that an institutionalized child is going to come with a list of challenges, regardless of its ethnicity. The problem is getting the word out to the people who wouldn't have chosen international adoption if Eastern Europe had remained closed. (A corollary belief: "love conquers all"—no matter what my child has been through, if I love him/her enough, he/she will be OK in the long run. This may be true for many children, but it's a bad premise upon which to found international adoption. Expect the best, but prepare for the worst!)

As far as why my kids' birth mothers relinquished them, all I can say is that the questioner would understand much better if they were to spend some time in Calcutta. People who haven't spent time in the third world simply have no clue what a birth mother there would be up against.

At times, Carol has been called a hero. It's a word she despises. "I absolutely hate it when people tell me what a wonderful person I am to take on these children. My children aren't perfect, but they're fundamentally happy, healthy, and handsome, and I didn't save their lives. The Indian orphanages did that." Saying that she's a wonderful person for adopting them implies that her children are undesirable, which is simply not the case. "Some of the same people who think of me as a 'hero' ask questions like, 'Couldn't you have any of your own children? Couldn't you get a white baby?'" This demeans Carol's children and enrages her. "I can handle garden-variety nosy people, but when they talk like that, I make a beeline in the opposite direction."

VIETNAM

Most aging "baby boomers" know at least something about Vietnam from the war. Some of us were affected directly through brothers and fathers going off to fight there; others can barely find it on a map. To Janice and Philip from Maine, Vietnam became a familiar place with the adoption of their two Vietnamese children. Already parents of two biological children, ages seven and four, the couple began to discuss the possibility of adoption. At first, they considered adopting a teenage girl. "A foster mother was our source of information. Then, after some soul-searching and observation of our oldest child's behavior, we decided to wait and adopt a child younger than our first one." Having two sons already, the couple was initially undecided whether to adopt a boy or a girl. When the pictures of the placements came—a worried-looking, thin, little five-year-old girl, and her frightened, angry-looking, four-year-old brother—the reality of what they were subjecting their biological kids to hit hard.

At the time, the agency was not encouraging parents to come and get their children in Vietnam. It was strictly done with escorts, who transferred the children from the orphanage to the United States. Because our children were older, I made it known that I really wanted to go get them. I felt it would be easier on the kids to meet me on their ground. I also wanted a chance to experience their culture. It was up and down. I really didn't know if I was going until a few days before I departed. My husband stayed home to take care of the older two, and I met a volunteer escort in Boston who was my travel companion for the next two weeks. I felt very anxious, nervous and adventurous!

Our first stop was in Bangkok, to get a visa to enter Vietnam. We were there for two days and flew into Hanoi the third day. Adrenalin flowed the entire time. I met my children the next day at the Giving and Receiving Ceremony. I gave them plenty of space to observe me and feel comfortable. I again was nervous, not really knowing what was expected of me. The Vietnamese like to give speeches, and I was asked to talk at the ceremony. I am not particularly eloquent, nor was I prepared; but I told them I was honored to be the mother of Van and Van (the children's Vietnamese names are the same, but pronounced differently). I promised to give them love, a family and an education. Once back at the hotel room, I bathed the kids and showed them the toys I brought, along with pictures of our home and family.

The rest of the week, Janice visited two orphanages and made seemingly endless trips to governmental offices to complete the necessary paperwork to leave the country. Her daughter, whom they chose to name Hannah, didn't enjoy going out of the hotel with her new mom because of all the attention she drew, naturally standing out in the crowd. After a grueling twenty-four-hour flight, complete with intestinal problems, the first weeks at home were total chaos. Hannah had crying jags that lasted up to two hours, often beginning at suppertime. The children have five older biological siblings still living in Vietnam. One night at bedtime, a few months after they arrived, Hannah said she was worried about her older brother. "He had walked a long way to bring the children to the people who would bring them to the orphanage. She asked my husband if he thought her brother made it back home." Janice and Philip naturally, feel a lot of compassion for the plight of the children's biological family and have told Hannah and Jake, the name they chose for the boy, that they may go back to visit Vietnam when they're older. Knowing that their biological mother has died, the couple has told the children that their mother is always with them as their angel.

In addition to Hannah's bouts of crying, Jake had temper tantrums, sometimes three or four a day. Janice was overwhelmed. Seeing her children's sadness, she questioned their decision to adopt them. Thankfully, by six weeks, the children were coping much better and beginning to settle into a routine. Janice was also coping better, and hired a high school student to help out. The couple has also been supported by their community, the school system, and their family and friends. "Partly," Janice stated, "because our children are very outgoing, and have enchanted everyone."

SOUTH AMERICA

Sarah and Jack, living in Maryland with their four children have experienced the joys of both domestic and international adoption. Three of their children are from South America. I asked Sarah if she had ever been called a hero.

"Yes, I've been called a hero. I don't really like it. It sounds as if I was looking for something else. The bottom line is we love kids." What influenced them to follow the path they did? What factors did they consider? And what types of children were she and her husband open to?

I went to international adoption because of such a long wait list for domestic adoptions. The first time we were domestically listed we waited two years, only to find out that an error was made and we weren't even on the list! We had to sign up again! Time went by and we kept checking our placement number, which, as we suspected, was hardly moving. Then we decided to contact an acquaintance to ask them how their international adoption went. After we learned of their positive experience, we decided to move in this direction. Whatever the agency had, we wanted to be notified. We'd even take twins. Soon thereafter, we were notified that two brothers from Colombia, were available for adoption. After we accepted our assignments, our families were as excited as we were. They kept giving me showers. You wouldn't have believed the toys we received! We could have opened a toy store.

After they got their boys, she and her husband were interested in adopting a girl. "There was a girl in Paraguay up for adoption. We said, 'great!' and started the paperwork." They ran into some difficulties, however. Apparently, Paraguay was inexperienced in handling international adoptions at the time. Nevertheless, Sarah and Philip paid for the child's living expenses for over a year, hearing in the meantime all sorts of reasons why it was taking so long. Then they were advised to sit back and wait to see what would develop.

While they waited, their lawyer contacted them with more good news—a girl was finally available for domestic adoption, but not the girl from Paraguay. They said yes.

We started coming up with girl names. Three days after he phoned, we dropped the boys off at grandma's and went to get our thirteen-day-old little baby girl. We were in shock. Smiles were stuck on our faces. We went home and called everyone saying we want you to come see something. They did, and everybody was laughing and crying all at the same time.

Then a few months later, the lawyer called again and asked if we still wanted the girl from Paraguay. 'Of course! She's our daughter, always, no matter where she was. I went to South America for three weeks and the poverty I saw was sickening. I give those people credit that decide not to have children because they know themselves better than we do. When she arrived in the states twelve years ago, our family was complete.

Now that her children are grown, dealing with her teenagers is not exactly what she expected. "It's very trying on the nerves."

Of course that has nothing to do with adoption. If you remember being a teen, then you probably remember saying, 'I wish I was never born.' But in the adopted world that's somewhat different. We hear more of, 'I wish I was never adopted.' We have tried to keep them informed of their cultures, but we were advised by the children to please help them be more like the children here. They don't want to be considered different. We feel that when they become adults it will be more of an interest to them. Their looks are the only thing they've had to deal with, and they've dealt with it in a good way—being very proud that they were 'chosen' and have lived in South America. All their friends think that is neat!

A One-And-A-Half Pound Baby Girl From Chile

Though not considered the norm, Lucy and Doug's adoption experience demonstrates some of the delays, disappointments and inaccurate information that can stall or sidetrack the adoption process. This story exemplifies what can be accomplished with perseverance. It's an adventure that eventually has a happy ending, bringing both a daughter and a son from Chile to a determined husband and wife.

The couple was married in 1980. It was Doug's second marriage and Lucy's first. Doug had four biological children from his first marriage, so the couple agreed not to have any more children. Seven years later, Doug changed his mind. 'Let's adopt,' he said to his wife. Though Lucy said there was some previous discussion about adoption in their family, they hadn't firmly decided that this was a path they would take. When they were certain, they selected Chile because they wanted a child who looked very different from themselves. "The number of countries available to us was very limited because of our ages," explained Lucy, who was forty-two, "but we also considered Thailand." Lucy gave an overview of their experiences and spoke about their despondency over their first failed assignment.

> To begin at the beginning for me would mean going back about eight years. Our second adoption took three-and-a-half years to complete. Our baby was given to another couple and the agency then had that couple contact us with pictures of the child. Our story is about living for twenty months with someone telling you that your child is coming home next month, and then finding out it's not really going to happen. It's about paying for foster care and then finding out that the attorney was keeping the money, even while the foster family couldn't afford medical care. It's about several trips to Chile and being interrogated by the courts because we were older parents. It's about a drunken attorney appearing in court. It's about being contacted by the Chilean attorney general, who is interested in putting the American agency out of business for 'unfair' practices.
>
> We heard that there was a little girl, one year old, who had some hearing difficulties. Would we take her? We said, 'Yes.' Later, however, the agency told us we couldn't, because the social worker who found this child had made a gross error. Our hearts were broken. What did we know? We'd never been through anything like this in our lives before.

Then, several months later they received a phone call about a baby girl five months old who was living in an orphanage, a girl born prematurely. The couple received her picture and complete medical background, though little was known about her parents' medical and genetic history. "When I saw her picture, I knew that I wanted her and nothing would stop me until I had her." The pediatricians advised them not to accept the assignment, feeling that she would never walk or talk. They felt she'd lead a far less than normal life.

> I was devastated. My husband arranged for us to meet with three additional pediatricians, a neonatologist, a neurologist and several other doctors. Their opinion, after extensive

review, was that environment would be everything in making this child healthy, and also the best of medical care. So we insisted we wanted her. She had cerebral palsy, suffered seizures, weighed only eight pounds by seven months of age, and was totally unhealthy.

In January of 1989 we called the attorney to see if we would be traveling soon. He said no. So we took a trip to Puerto Rico to take our minds off the waiting. A week later when we arrived home, we were greeted with a letter telling us to come to Chile as soon as possible to pick up our daughter. When we arrived in Chile, we went to court first thing that day, and two hours later made the trip to the orphanage to see our daughter for the first time! The Chilean orphanages keep the children until they are ten years old and then put them out onto the streets if they have not been adopted. This is done so that if the biological parents want them back, they have ten years to do it.

At the orphanage we were brought into a room and made to wear sterile gowns. After that they brought our daughter. I was in tears from happiness. She was so tiny my husband couldn't touch her for fear of hurting her. I just looked at her, took her clothes off, and examined her all over, counted her fingers and toes, just as any mother would.

They went to court once again two days later, then back to the orphanage to pick up their daughter. Once there, they found themselves hopelessly waiting. Apparently, there was some concern that the baby's biological mother had come back to take her home. Lucy remembered her surprise, "What? No, they can't do this after all this time. Just give me my baby and let me out of here." Eventually the mix up was explained. When they were able to walk through the orphanage, they found its conditions deplorable. They were taken to their daughter's room, and were horrified at the sight. Inside one room, thirty babies were being tended to by only one nurse. "Our daughter was tied in her bed and had never been out of it. They fed her with a bottle with a nipple as big as a house, so they could feed these babies faster," said Lucy. "My daughter never learned to suck!"

From there the couple went to an American doctor who said he would sign the papers for the child to leave the country:

We were required to be in Chile a total of fourteen days. In a small room with a new baby, this was the pits. Her formula was rice, sugar and boiling hot water. You had to mix it and then shake it. Unfortunately, the agency recommended we bring the disposable feeding bags. While I was shaking one of these, it exploded from the heat. Formula everywhere! We immediately went out and bought plastic bottles. We also had to bring new clothes for her to the orphanage as they wouldn't let her leave with a thing. Nothing. Not even a blanket or diaper.

During 1989, Chile was attempting to overthrow its leader, Pinochet. Their hotel was directly across from the Royal Palace. Armed guards were noticeable everywhere—on the streets, in the parks, in the shops. Then their daughter was sick with diarrhea and suffering from malnutrition. She had a severe diaper rash all the way up to her neck. In addition, the child was filthy when Lucy and her husband picked her up from the orphanage. The new mom scrubbed for two days to clean the crud from her ears, while the child screamed pitifully. Apparently she had never been bathed before.

Remember, this is our first adoption. "The second one was worse!" I thought nothing could be as bad. Just some background information on my daughter: She weighed only one-and-a-half pounds at birth. Consequently, she was in the hospital for a month, then sent to the orphanage. She was there three days and was sent back to the hospital where she was put on a respirator for thirty-one days. She was sent back to the orphanage in good health, was there for two days, and back to the hospital with a full body infection. She was transfused, kept for two weeks, sent back to the orphanage, back to the hospital, and finally was back in the orphanage when we picked her up.

When we arrived home, my husband's ninety-two-year-old mother was waiting for us. By the way, we did not get any support when we told the family we were adopting. We were told we were crazy. My husband's mother especially thought we were nuts. But she was there waiting. She had to see this baby. We told her that we were naming her after her, and she replied, 'What do you want to do that for?' We did anyway, and let me tell you, this child gave her more enjoyment in her life-time than any other grandchild. Everyone was so against us initially, but then was so supportive. After rounds with the pediatrician, we discovered our daughter was worse off than we had imagined. They had discontinued her phenobarbital in Chile when we picked her up, and she began having seizures every thirty minutes. The first year was hell. No one would baby-sit because they were afraid. But I didn't give up. We got the best medical care, including EKGs, CAT scans, and so on. Where we live, the state has to support children at risk, and I brought her to the developmentalists. In one year, no one could believe the change in this little girl. She began walking and laughing! Our whole community celebrated in the life of the child. Even the pediatrician who said she would never walk or talk came to visit us.

Here I was with this little baby, my first, and she was so small and sick. Her formula cost us $95.00 a week. We had to special order it at the pharmacy. She wouldn't eat, and I had to wake her every four hours to feed her. If she took an ounce at a time, we were lucky. And she wouldn't grow. At one year of age, she weighed only twelve pounds. She didn't talk until she was three years old.

Lucy spoke of some of her daughter's lingering behaviors that stemmed from her early upbringing in the orphanage.

The only really unusual behavior my daughter exhibits now is that she will not sleep on her stomach. That was how she was tied in bed. Even as a baby when she first came home, she wouldn't sleep on her stomach. Other than that, she was really too young when she came home to exhibit anything, except that she has an extreme attachment to me. The pediatrician indicated that these children know something happened to them, even as young as seven months of age, though they don't know what. She was very terrified if you accidentally waved your hand in front of her face. I think she was struck as an infant. Also she doesn't cry much, probably because she learned that crying in the orphanage did little good.

Lucy isn't certain if she and her husband will have to go through life defending their decision to adopt cross culturally. But she is certain that she's prepared to go through her life defending her children's right to be here, to be Catalan Spanish, to be adopted, and to be citizens of the United States. Two of her daughter's "best friends" told her that she was a throw-away baby and that her mother didn't want her. "I was in an uproar." Lucy said, "This did not come from her friends, but from their parents!" Her daughter thought about these comments all last summer. Then one day she said, "I know you're my real mother because if you were my fake mother, you'd be plastic and you aren't." Previously, Lucy had told her daughter that her real mother was the woman she lived with. And that, yes, there was another woman to whom she was born. "One summer we were at the beach. My little girl was about two years old. Her hair was very curly. An older woman came up to me to tell me how much she loved 'mulatto' children and she would love to meet my black husband. I pointed at my husband, who was across the way. He's very light-skinned and has red hair—very Irish. She was so embarrassed."

EAGER FOR A SIBLING

Lucy and Doug were eager to adopt a sibling for their daughter, so they began the adoption process again in 1990 by contacting the same agency. They completed their home study with a social worker who happened to live on the next street. "She went through our house with white gloves and insisted on interviewing our daughter alone, though she couldn't yet talk," explained Lucy. They then contacted the same attorney and sent their adoption papers off. Three months later, they were notified that this attorney was not dealing in adoptions any longer. The agency picked another attorney for the couple, an attorney who insisted upon $3,000 of his $11,000 total fee up front.

Then it started. We got called for a little boy. We said 'Yes.' Two months later we were told the birth mother changed her mind and wasn't putting the boy up for adoption. A month later another call, another boy. Pictures were sent. We got a call from the agency that this, too, was falling through. Two months later, I got a call from a couple who were traveling to pick up their child. 'What is Chile like?', they asked. I gave them as much information as I could and told them to keep in touch. Well, they returned, and called us to say that this little boy was supposed to be ours, but they got him instead because they were younger.

Then before Christmas, we had another child, with pictures. But this one also fell through. Lo and behold, we went to the agency Christmas party and there was a second couple with our second assignment! I couldn't stand this. I was a basket case. We insisted on communication with the attorney. We talked to him and he wanted more money. His fee had increased to $15,000. A few months later, we got a little girl. Again, the birth mother changed her mind. Six months later we got a little boy: he is six months old, will we take him? Yes! He will be home by the time he is eight months old. Yes!! Yes!! But the child was being put in foster care during the court proceedings. We were to pay $250 per month for this care and send children's clothing to the attorney. In the meantime, we got another call from the attorney. This time he told us that it would start costing $350 per month for foster care.

I purchased an airline ticket to coincide with the date I was given. Then we'd get a phone call telling us of a delay. This went on, month after month, for ten months. In the meantime, other people were traveling to pick up their children. I finally called the attorney myself and told him I was coming. I told him when I was leaving and how long I would be staying in Chile. He'd better have the two court dates that I needed to get my child out of the country. In all this time, we never received another picture of our son, no medicals, absolutely nothing. It was a very trying time. Meanwhile, my daughter and everyone else wanted to know when our baby was coming home. My son was now sixteen months old. When I told family and friends that I was going to Chile, this time by myself, they thought I was crazy. So I made my flight reservations, booked an apartment this time, got in touch with one of my friends and hired an interpreter. I contacted the attorney again and told him I would be arriving at such-a-such time and place, and to please have arrangements in place to pick me up at the airport. Grudgingly, he said he would, if I arrived with the final payment due him.

In the meantime, I wrote a letter to the foster mother (whom I knew nothing about) and had it translated into Spanish. I wrote to let her know how difficult all this must have been for her and how difficult it must be to give up the boy she'd taken care of for so long. If she wanted to write a letter to the child, I told her I would put it away and let him read it on his eighteenth birthday. I also told her that I was forever indebted to her. I knew nothing about this woman, her family, her living conditions, how my son was cared for—nothing. I arrived in Santiago after a twenty-hour flight. I was on a plane so small that I doubted it would make it to the next city, never mind halfway around the world. In less than three hours after arriving, I met my son. Three women rang my room bell and walked in with him. God, he was beautiful! So handsome! And so-o-o-big. I figured out which one was the foster mother. They were all trying to get this little boy to go see his new 'Mamma' while he would have nothing to do with me. I told them, 'Please don't rush him. Let us have a chance to know one another.' I brought out some bubbles. This is the way to every young child's heart. I had him amused. He hugged me, smiled and laughed.

I turned to the attorney and asked him if I could give the foster mother my letter. He looked at it, noticed that it was in Spanish, and said, 'Yes.' I then handed a gift to the foster mother. She cried. The attorney yelled at her in Spanish and pushed her out the door. He turned to me and said that the child was mine until the court date in the morning. Then I was alone with my son, who immediately started screaming at the top of his lungs. I had nothing in the apartment to give him—no milk, no food. He wouldn't stop screaming, screaming, screaming, so I decided to go out to the supermarket.

He was sixteen months old and weighed over thirty-five pounds. He couldn't walk. So I carried him in the elevator down to the main floor and up a flight of stairs to the street.

I put him down. He rolled and crawled into the middle of the street, where he sat and screamed and screamed. I managed to attract the doorman's attention, to let him know that I needed help getting this child back into my apartmento. He carried this screaming, kicking, hitting child back to my apartment, and left. Meanwhile, my son would not be quiet. I called the interpreter and asked her to buy some groceries. Before she arrived, I had all the tenants banging their walls to be 'silento,' while my son continued to scream. The interpreter arrived with the food. Then she, too, had to go for she 'can't listen to it any longer.' I took my son and put him on the floor, where he collapsed and continued to scream even louder. By now my phone was ringing. It was the owner of the apartment building telling me I must quiet him. I couldn't. My son crawled under a chair like a frightened animal and screamed for five hours straight! Yes, five hours! I timed it. I felt very sorry for him. He had no idea what was going on. The only mother he knew left him with a stranger, who did not even speak the same language. He finally fell asleep from exhaustion.

Later, when he awoke, I talked to him in a soothing voice while I took his clothes off for a bath. Oh no! Big mistake! He cried and clutched his blue jeans. He would not let them go. I said, what the hell. Let him take them in the tub. He cried some more and refused to sit down in the tub. I took him out with sopping wet jeans and put on his new pajamas. He felt the pajamas over and over again with both hands and seemed to like them. (I realized later that the jeans were the only clothes he'd ever had, and he'd never had a bath before because the foster mom didn't have running water in the house.) I put him to bed—no longer screaming, but perfectly happy. Thank God. So much for the first day with my son!

To adopt successfully, parents must be willing to give up their egos and any thoughts that they will have a child like them, either in looks or personality. They must be able to accept the child they have, no matter what. "They must be a fighter for what they really want," Lucy added, "and be able to visualize the future."

[1] From the National Adoption Information Clearinghouse, Box 1182, Washington, D.C. 20013-1182; 703-352-3488 or 888-251-0075; www.calib.com/naic

CHAPTER 7

Domestic Experiences and Other Insights

Dear Special Person:

Our hearts go out to you as you are making one of the toughest and most sensitive decisions in your life. We know you have given this great thought because of the deep love you have for your baby....Words alone can never fully express what your decision will mean to us, but we promise you will feel at peace if you choose us. Your baby will be raised in a loving, warm and caring home. We look forward to hearing from you.

—Excerpt from one adoptive couple's
'Dear Birth Mom' letter

AS WITH INTERNATIONAL ADOPTIONS, DOMESTIC ADOPTIONS CAN BE facilitated with the help of an agency, although sometimes an adopting couple or individual is frustrated by the law of supply and demand. Many individuals are looking for healthy Caucasian infants to complete their families and at times, there simply aren't enough for immediate placement. Every year, according to the Gladney Center for Adoption, approximately 1 million teens from fifteen to nineteen years old become pregnant. Fifty percent of these women choose to parent, and forty-eight percent terminate their pregnancy. Only two percent choose an adoption plan. Consequently, more and more prospective adoptive parents are writing their own 'Dear Birth Mom' letters, placing ads in local and national newspapers, and using a variety of other means to help them locate expectant mothers, mothers who might be thinking of putting their babies up for adoption and are unsure of where to turn. Though they can be time consuming and emotionally draining, efforts like these can be successful. Speaking directly with expectant moms about their wishes and needs, however, can leave a person feeling extremely vulnerable. One couple I interviewed installed a separate telephone line into their home so they wouldn't miss a call. In addition, it's not unheard of for one of the spouses to quit his or her job in order to be available to answer the phone. "Who would want to miss even one phone call by not being there? Expectant moms might never call back," said a father of two adopted boys living in Detroit.

Parents like Paul and Suzie, who met on a blind date, plan to contact expectant mothers by displaying their biographical flyers in every imaginable place. "Different individuals have come up with clever places to hang them for us," she explained, "such as maternity wards, libraries, supermarkets, church halls and YMCAs. We have postings up all around the country." Hiring a private attorney who can assist in locating a child is another method used by singles and couples pursuing domestic adoption.

The waiting period for the finalization of a domestic adoption varies widely from state to state. Some states require a two-day waiting period; other states, like New York, have in the past required a forty-five day period. Domestic adoptions differ from international adoptions, in part, by the nature of the contact between birth parents and adoptive parents and adopted children. Domestic adoptions can either be closed, semi-open, or open, depending upon the agreement signed by the birth parents. Some birth parents cherish full contact with adoptive parents and find these types of relationships very satisfying. Others, after considering their options, decide to limit or have no contact with their biological child and adoptive family. One of the reasons I heard for deciding to adopt domestically was a strong desire to locate a child of similar race. For a number of parents, that meant reaching out to children with disadvantages—children with disabilities of all sorts, hard-to-place sibling groups, and older children.

Domestic adoptions, like international adoptions, are sometimes clouded by negative publicity. A handful of recent stories that received heavy media coverage, for example, included photographs of tearful adoptive families being torn apart by reemerging biological parents. In cases like these, the rights of birth parents and adoptive parents can become temporarily blurred. It can be a devastating experience for the adoptive parents and disruptive for the adopted child. One person suggested that birth parents who reappear should have to pay a type of alimony. Yet, for the number of domestic adoptions in which the biological parents do return to take their child, there are thousands more with happier endings. Domestic adoptions, including those with single, gay, and lesbian adoptive parents, have worked wonderfully for the vast majority who chose to share their experiences.

A PRIVATE ADOPTION STORY

Various factors influence singles and couples who pursue an adoption within the United States. A deep attachment to their Italian heritage was one such factor for Tony and Maria of Staten Island. Adopting a child outside of their ethnicity was not an acceptable option. They both knew prior to their marriage that biological children would not be possible. Without hesitation, they decided to pursue the adoption of two children. Now they have a wonderful four-year-old daughter, and more recently have adopted a boy. In fact, before the adoption of their son, Maria asked me if I'd help in their private adoption search by displaying their one-page biography at our local YMCA. Their biography is an example of what birth mothers review in looking for a family.

Dear Special Person,

Allow us to tell you about ourselves: we live on a tree-lined street in a suburban community where we built our home with three bedrooms and a large fenced-in backyard. In May, we adopted Anna, our precious daughter, who has brought great happiness and joy to our hearts and home. With still one empty bedroom and a backyard filled with swings, slides and many toys waiting to be shared, our family will not be complete until we are fortunate enough to adopt another bundle of joy.

Our daughter eagerly awaits a sister or brother. Each day she says something special in anticipation that it will happen soon. She has drawn pictures and has put aside toys and stuffed animals to give to the baby when he or she comes home. Thinking about the future birth of that special baby brings tears to my eyes. As adults we pray and wait for that glorious day, but to hear it from an almost four-year-old really tears at our hearts.

My husband, Tony, a funeral director and a compassionate person, is actively involved in caring for our daughter and will be a hands-on dad with our new baby. I am a mom and wife, which I thoroughly enjoy. We both have loving and supportive extended families with whom we are very close. I have one married sister with two young sons and Tony has one married brother.

As a family, we enjoy gatherings, outings, Sunday Mass. Belonging to an adopting parents support group has helped us become a stronger family and has provided us with a fine way to share and to learn how to talk with our daughter about adoption. She loves to read with us and many of her storybooks explain her roots. To this day, her birth parents continue to remind us of the peace they gained by choosing us as her parents. We have discussed with them our plans to adopt again, and their response was, 'Ask the birth parents to speak to us, because we have no doubt that you are wonderful parents.'

As words alone can never explain or express what your decision will mean to us, we promise you will feel at peace if you were to choose us. Your baby will be raised in a loving, warm and caring home. Thanks for listening to our story. We know it is difficult to get to know someone from a letter, so we would be honored and look forward to hearing from you.'

Maria and Tony selected their first agency because of its longevity. "They had more than eighty-six years in the family services business," she explained, "initially starting out as a foster-child placement agency. In addition, the agency had a deep concern about providing counseling for the birth moms. "Counseling for birth moms is extremely important." Did she have any regrets? Her reply was simply, "No."

Emotional Hardship and Unfair Scrutiny

For Henry and his wife of fifteen years, Gloria, the adoption of their infant son came about after being told of their infertility. For Henry, the grieving period that followed that prognosis was short-lived. "In fact," he began, "I told my wife that I was willing to adopt as we were leaving the doctor's office after getting the news." By his own admission, their son is the greatest thing that has ever happened to them, but that doesn't mean he wasn't frustrated with the adoption process—specifically, the unfair scrutiny of prospective adopted parents. No biological parent, he noted, undergoes the kind of magnifying glass examination adoptive parents do.

We thought long, hard and carefully about adoption. In the fall of '94, we decided adoption was for us. We were accepted by a small adoption agency in our home state in January '95. Our son was placed in our home in March of '96. He's the best thing that has ever happened to us. We live in Texas, which, at that time, required a forty-eight hour waiting period after the birth of a child before the birth parents can sign a relinquishment of parental rights. Our son's birth mom and dad kept him for that entire time period. His birth parents were hoping to 'give him a better chance' through adoption. We did adopt a child of our race. That was important to us from a cultural, not racial, standpoint. My frustration was, and is, over the fact that adoptive families are put in a position of having to prove they are fit to parent. Had we been able to have biological children, no one would have put us under the same scrutiny.

I understand that the state and adoption agencies must exercise care in the placement of children. Adoptive families, however, are not second-class citizens and we shouldn't have to prove our fitness to parent. The inability to conceive a biological child should not create a presumption of the inability to parent. Likewise, it should not be presumed that a person who is capable of conceiving a biological child is naturally fit to parent.

"WHY IS IT SO EASY FOR EVERYONE ELSE TO HAVE A BABY AND SO VERY HARD FOR ME?"

That was the perplexing question Ruth was asking herself. She admits to being jealous when she found herself in the company of pregnant women while she was trying so desperately to have a biological child.

Jealousy doesn't even begin to describe the feeling of seeing pregnant women. I would see or hear of someone who was pregnant, very young and not married, and who was going to keep the baby. I remember others around me at that time were popping out a couple of babies one right after the other. My husband, Al, and I would be invited to birthday parties for different people's kids and I wouldn't go because I couldn't stand to be around that situation. After you're married a few years lots of people start asking you when you're going to start a family. Was it really any of their business?

After we got on the list, we would buy something for the baby once in awhile and I would keep calling the agency and bugging them. Finally, a few years after our first contact they seemed to indicate it probably wouldn't be much longer. We started going to classes on adoption and the care of babies through Catholic Charities.

I will never forget the day we received our call. I was cleaning the tub when I answered the phone at about 9:30 that morning. It was mid-April. I remember every word our social worker said, and I remember telling my husband the news. We weren't supposed to pick up the baby until 2 P.M. in a city about sixty miles away. Can you imagine, my husband stayed at work until noon?

What do you take to your first meeting with your daughter? We didn't know what size diapers because we didn't know how big she was. We knew she was four weeks old, but how many pounds is that? I remember buying a diaper pail. I never did use that thing. On the ride over we discussed the name. Then the time came. We walked into the foster parents' house and there she was: the most perfect little girl sitting in her infant seat in the middle of the bed in the cutest little pink dress. I cried!

Then I counted fingers and toes. Just perfect. So the time came to leave. They asked if we brought a blanket to take her home in. It was also raining, and we had no umbrella. All the stuff we brought—no blanket! Then the next problem. The car seat. How do you operate this thing? That was really funny. We had three people in the back seat trying to figure it out.

Ruth described her first hours with their newly adopted baby and the many questions she had to answer.

As soon as we walked into our house, I could smell something. Oh, No! What do I do? I have to change the baby. I tried to talk Al into it but he didn't want any part of it. Then we called the grandparents to tell them we were home. We all lived in the same very small town of about one hundred people. I'm an only child, so this was my parents' first grandbaby. They were so excited. The baby started fussing. I bet she's hungry. So I went to mix some formula. I was mixing water-formula. Got my fork and I was mixing, mixing. How come there are clumps in the formula? Why isn't it dissolving? Hmmmmmm. Oh, well. Days later I learned that you are supposed to boil the water before mixing. Duh!

Now that she's become a parent, she offered this suggestion to potential parents: put your names on agency waiting lists long before you think you're ready.

Adoption is such a very special kind of love. I think the only advice I could give someone who is trying to conceive on their own and having fertility problems is to look into adoption before all the tests are done, and before that final doctor visit. Put your names in just in case that ends up being the road you'll take, because the wait can be so very long. If they call you before you're ready, you can always say no. That would be the only thing I would have done differently. The only thing I regret is not being able to meet our daughter's birth mom. All I know is that both her parents were in college. We did get to meet our son's birth mom and it was the most incredible experience ever. There are so very many questions I have about our daughter and her unique personality. I call her a very spirited little girl. A lot of these questions are answered at these face to face meetings with the biological mother. We still keep in touch with my son's. My wish is that someday both our children will want to search. I would have no problems with that at all.

Thoughts on Open and Semi-Open Adoptions

Both of Jill and Dan's children's adoptions are considered open, but the degree of that openness continually varies. Jill stated her impressions of open adoptions.

There are so many degrees of openness that I don't think you can have one general definition. Both of our children's adoptions are considered open, but they are very different. With our oldest, Edward, who is now six, we first met his birth mom when he was two months old. We felt an immediate trust and exchanged addresses. We see her once or twice each year, when she usually stays with us. With our daughter, who is three, her birth mom didn't want to meet us at birth, though I corresponded with her monthly for the first year.

For a Caucasian couple now living in Alaska, the experiences of both open and semi-open adoption have enriched their lives, though friends and family initially rejected the idea. "There were a few people that thought we were nuts for being open and meeting our son's birth mom," began Carol. "Even virtual strangers seem to have trouble with the fact that I was in the delivery room at the time of his birth." Carol straightforwardly detailed her unproductive medical treatments by both military and civilian doctors prior to adopting their two children, both of whom, are one-half native Alaskans.

At the time, my husband Michael was on active duty with the Air Force and our medical care was provided by the military's medical system. From Texas, he and I moved to Utah, then he moved to Turkey, then we both ended up in Spain. As I recall, my husband had a couple of sperm counts done. The first one was less than wonderful but the next one was better—after making adjustments in underwear and temperature of bath water. Then I had gas infused into my system to see if my tubes were clear—they were.

After that, this wonderful doctor suggested I was just too high strung to get pregnant, so he put me on phenobarbitol to calm down. We left Spain after three years and moved back to the States.

I was referred to a doctor in the civilian community. He saw me once in his office, then he suggested and scheduled laproscopic surgery to view my pelvic area. The next time I saw him was in the hospital. He asked my age (twenty-six or twenty-seven at the time) and then asked something along the lines of 'you don't want children?' I nearly jumped out of the bed. I reminded him that I was an infertility patient. He said, 'Oh,' and rearranged his surgery schedule putting me at the end, instead of at the beginning. I believe he would have done a tubal ligation on me that day if I hadn't been alert. At this point it had been more than five years since we began pursuing our dream. I was fed up with being treated like a piece of meat. I went through a period of deep depression, which required medication and counseling. That occurred in the eighth year of our marriage. I refer to it as my 'winter of discontent.'

Then Carol and Michael began exploring the possibility of adopting. One agency told her husband that he was too old to adopt, another said that since they both had been divorced, they weren't eligible. "The only one that would talk to us was in El Salvador, and that country was on the no-no list for military personnel. We felt we were out of luck. Then we started talking about private adoption. This seemed like a much better option." Eventually, the couple had their adoptions completed, their two children—and the family of their dreams.

In Defense

Elizabeth is another woman who experienced infertility, and, like some other adoptive parents, also had to tolerate the insensitive, upsetting remarks of fertile women. One woman asked Elizabeth if she thought her husband would have married her if he had known that she couldn't give him his own child. Another woman told her that she had taken the easy way out because she didn't have to go through child birth. She introduced me to the term triad, which refers to the adopted children, their biological parents and their adoptive parents.

I've had four operations because of my endometriosis; the last one was a hysterectomy. None of these were as painful as not being able to get pregnant. We had concerns with the baby's birth parents' health. We did not want to accept a child if either of their medical histories were unknown, or if the child was a result of rape. Personally, I couldn't handle that. When we were ready to pursue adoption, we wanted to know the background of the birth parents for two reasons. First, so we were sure the birth mom had proper prenatal care and wasn't taking drugs or using alcohol. And second, because we feel it's important for our children to know where they came from. At the beginning of the process we had a problem with open adoption, but after research and attending seminars, we realized that it was in the best interest of all triad members.

In preparing for their home study, she and her husband Kevin had different reactions. Elizabeth felt that it was an important process of personal discovery; to him, it was an invasion of privacy. "I realized the politics in adoption. I'm convinced that because I had such a good relationship with our social worker we got our children faster. Face it, people work better for people they like." Their toughest assignment was writing their 'Dear Birth Mom' letter, offering an intimate description of their home, security, moral structure and parenting beliefs in hopes to connect with the wishes of an expectant woman. Elizabeth added, "We put a lot of thought into ours. This is what all the birth moms look at to make their big decisions."

How did Elizabeth and her husband feel about their choice to accept an open adoption, I wondered, now that they had their children? Did they find they had to defend that choice over and over? As I became more familiar with adoption groups on the internet, that seemed like a distinct possibility. Often in these electronic exchanges, the views of open adoption were very opinionated and, at times, bluntly antagonistic. Sadly, I also became increasingly familiar with the seemingly large amount of hostility coming from grown adopted children. Some of them, apparently, were having to defend their lives as adopted children, or simply felt lost, while others harbored hostilities stemming from feelings of low self-esteem or of not belonging. One anonymous adopted young adult agonized over being called a bastard. Elizabeth talked about the misunderstanding and fears that can cloud open adoptions.

> The only time I feel that I have to defend adoption is when I say, 'open.' Some people don't understand what's involved with an open adoption. When our son's birth mom comes to visit, I don't tell anyone except my parents. At times the visits are a little uncomfortable, but I feel it's in the best interest of our son. His birth mom also has a baby that she is now parenting, and he loves to spend time with her. I do wonder when he'll figure out that this is his half sister, but I never think about either birth mom taking our kids back.
>
> Since they chose us through letters, they had control of who parented their children. This gives me the security I need. I think most people don't understand open adoption because of the few cases in the media in the last few years. But if you study the cases, they were all private adoptions. Perhaps the birth parents didn't go through counseling before or after. In those cases, I feel that the attorneys were intent on making a placement. I feel that most of the problems could have been avoided if there had been proper counseling before placement. Also, it's my understanding that once the adoption is final, the birth parents cannot take children back. In all the cases I've heard about, the adoptions were not finalized because the birth parents protested relinquishment early in placement.
>
> Our kids have known they were adopted from day one. I

began talking to our kids about their adoption when they were just little babies. It's so natural to them. They assume everyone was adopted. Our son used to ask friends whose tummy they came out of. In fact, a year ago we were having dinner with friends, and the wife was eight months pregnant. Our son asked them who they were going to give their baby to. The poor couple just sat there not knowing what to say to him. I really don't understand people who don't tell their children they're adopted. If you're secretive and ashamed, they'll feel the same way. I heard my son teasing his friend once, saying, "ha, ha, ha...I came out of someone else's tummy and you came out of your mommy's."

COMMENTARY ON CLOSED ADOPTIONS

Lauren and Joseph adopted an African American child through closed adoption. The couple began attempting to conceive shortly after they were married, then, two years into their marriage, Lauren had a partial hysterectomy, leaving them with two options: in vitro fertilization or adoption. Considering the success rate, and the emotional and the physical risk of multiple births, they decided upon adoption. They began by researching agencies all over Maine, including nonprofit agencies, private agencies and the Department of Human Services. After reviewing all the information, they found Maine Adoption Placement Service to be the most nonjudgmental, liberal and caring agency available. "Everyone was supportive of our decision, although we were not seeking approval from them."

She described the emotional moment when she held their son for the first time at Boston International Airport.

He was four weeks old when we were told by the agency to pick him up. We were incredibly nervous, but excited. When his plane arrived, he was brought to us by the escort who had flown with him. I was jumping up and down and crying. I had been holding him for almost five minutes when my husband said, "I'd like to hold him too!" I was so glad to hold our son that I was not even paying attention to anyone else.

Although their agreement doesn't allow for any relationship with the biological mother, they have treasured pictures of their son while he was in the care of a foster family.

WITH THE HELP OF AN ATTORNEY

For Julie, forty-two, and her husband Ted, forty-seven, their first thoughts about adopting a child in order to create their family were distant and somewhat ambivalent. After numerous unsuccessful fertility treatments, adopting was an idea they were not eager to embrace: it meant giving up. When they eventually did decide to pursue a domestic adoption, it came about rather suddenly with a surprise phone call from Julie's sister. Though it happened more than twelve years ago, the events and emotions of their first of four adoptions is still fresh in Julie's mind.

> Ted, my husband, is from a tiny town in Alabama and grew up during the time of the civil rights movement. I'm from a town along the beach in Southern California in San Diego County. We were engaged for three months when Ted told me he didn't like the crowded conditions of California and would I consider relocating to settle and raise a family? I agreed. He then interviewed in Portland, Oregon, and we have been here for the past seventeen years, and we love it! It's been a great spot to raise our children. We live in a house with a huge front porch we built eight years ago. We live at the end of a cul-de-sac, so the kids can ride their bikes and skates without any traffic. Better Homes and Gardens even came and photographed our house once. After two years, we were ready to have our own family. We were surprised when I became pregnant so suddenly. Soon, however, it was obvious that something was terribly wrong and I miscarried. After that, I felt like an emotional wreck every time I saw a baby. As time went by, we decided to try again.

Julie unfortunately, miscarried again. This time, she said, she hadn't let herself get so emotionally involved. The doctors diagnosed her with having endometriosis. She remembers crying herself to sleep at night pleading for a baby. Looking back, that period was the hardest time in their married life. In the summer of that year their spirits were lifted by a call from Julie's sister, who was a nurse in Illinois. She explained that a pregnant woman had approached her and asked if she wanted to adopt her baby.

> At the time, my sister told the woman that she had a sister in Oregon who might be interested. It was unheard of to have a baby come to you. When she called, I told her that we'd think about it and call her back the next day. We hadn't even talked about adopting prior to that. We talked to our pastor, and asked, 'What would you do?' and his answer was, 'Pray!' So we did, and by the next day, we were ready to call back and tell her 'Yes!' Once we made that decision, we got very excited knowing that God had worked this miracle for us. The baby was due in three months. When we agreed, we hired an attorney in Illinois to handle that end and called another attorney in Oregon. As we were able to more or less follow the birth mom's progress via my sister, my relationship with my sister grew closer and closer. This was another of God's ways to bring us together.

Julie flew to Illinois to pick up their new daughter and fell in love with her immediately. "The hospital treated me like I had given birth myself," she told me. "I brought her home on my 31st birthday, and Ted had organized a coming home party. We settled easily into being parents. I loved playing mommy and she was an easy baby."

Since they really wanted more children, Julie and Ted decided to contact the attorney who had handled their daughter's adoption. Several months later, they were notified that the attorney had a good match for them and they soon had another addition to their family. She recalled the events of the day her new daughter arrived, a day filled with friends dropping by to visit their new addition. Later in the day she was suddenly gripped by pain.

> At 2:30 A.M. my husband called one of the doctors who lived next door to us and I was taken to the hospital. To make a horrible night's story short, it turned out that I had another tubal

pregnancy rupture. (I didn't even know I was pregnant!) They performed major surgery to stop the bleeding. I had hardly any time with our new daughter, so Ted would sneak her into me at night so I could hold her.

They subsequently went on to adopt another child, their third. "One morning the attorney's wife came to our home holding a huge bouquet of blue flowers and announced that we had a boy. We settled upon a name and we picked him up from the hospital two days later. We fell in love with him too." Julie added that it's been great fun having a boy in the family. "He's a little sweetie, and in kindergarten this year. Around Christmas, I kept getting a thought in my head that said, 'get a brother for our son.'" Her girls were only twenty months apart in age and were especially close. She had always felt like their son was left out, until, that is, they began to consider their fourth adoption. Julie's friend, a director of an adoption agency, informed them of a four-year-old boy living in Russia. They plan on adding him to their family in the near future.

For another couple, attorneys facilitated both of their domestic adoptions. Jill worked as a computer programmer prior to becoming a full-time mom, while George, her husband, was working as a sales manager. They enjoy relaxing by hiking, camping, canoeing and inviting friends and family over to their home. She shared some of her advice for people considering adoption:

First, talk with people who have adopted to find out what worked for them and what didn't. I'm amazed when people say that there aren't enough children out there to be adopted. Look for agencies that are placing a larger number of children. While you're in the adoption process, keep a journal and a calendar of your experiences. It will be a great tool to show your child how much they are loved. Other advice, if a linkup doesn't work out, don't stop—keep going. There will be a child for you.

Thoughts on Bonding

Many parents have already touched upon a very important issue—bonding. Health-care professionals know that forming an intimate relationship with one other person, and then learning to separate from that one person, is one of the most significant experiences that a human being, especially an infant, can have. It's referred to as a symbiotic relationship. I was so concerned about forming a symbiotic relationship with our baby, that I phoned a child psychologist in St. Louis even before we accepted our assignment. "If we're given a choice in adopting an infant or an older child, say, two years of age," I asked her, "what would you suggest from a bonding stand point?"

The psychologist replied, "I feel that the most formative years in a child's life are the first two. During that time, many lessons are learned, lessons that are carried throughout life. One lesson is trust. While I can't offer you an opinion, I can recommend some things to do once you bring the child home, things to make the adjustment period easier." Her advice was very direct.

I would keep his or her room simple. No dangling mobiles, not a lot of bright colors, not a lot of stuffed animals, no matter how tempting. You want the child to focus on your face and not be distracted. I would also recommend keeping friends and relatives away for two weeks or so, until the child settles into its new environment. And I wouldn't take the child anywhere and leave him or her there without you, for at least three months. That means no baby sitter. If Grandma and Grandpa want to come see the baby, have them come to your house, don't go to theirs.

In most families, the development of this intimate relationship usually occurs between the infant and his or her birth parents in the first few months of age, until the child learns to separate. Developmentally, this separation slowly begins to occur, around the age of seven or eight months, when the child begins to crawl, and continues throughout childhood. When a child is adopted at a later age, however, be it twelve months or thirty, that stage of total dependence has passed. Adoptive parents consequently, need to know as much as possible about their child's earliest experiences, not only chronologically, but also developmentally and psychologically.

I asked some adoptive parents, and also some individuals who were waiting to adopt, if they felt there was a difference between bonding with a biological child and bonding with an adopted child; many said no. Others, like Annette, who worked as an obstetric nurse, qualified their responses, noting that there are some differences, but that the differences are not necessarily negative or detrimental. Annette sees the differences, instead, as being subtle:

> I think the difference is that women who carry a child for nine months already have formed some kind of bond with their child. When adopting, one day you're childless, and the next day you're a family. There are so many new things—schedules, emotions, just getting used to having someone else to think about. Bonding occurs, but it comes with a little longer time span. Also, in some ways I feel I went through labor with with my adopted children in going through the process of adoption.

Annette and her husband, Matt, spent four years attempting to cope with the range of emotions associated with their undiagnosed infertility, including hopelessness, anger and desperation. She remembers the pain of feeling as if she had slid a little deeper into a black hole every time the doctors didn't find anything wrong. Not surprisingly then, the first time Annette held her adopted child she felt that a whole new world lay ahead of her and her family.

> With our first child, the timing couldn't have been better. My brother was getting married in Kansas City on May 14, a Saturday. Our family was leaving the morning of the 13th to be there. My other brother and his family had flown in from San Diego, so we were all busy running errands, shopping, and making last-minute arrangements. Things hadn't been going well for me that day. I was behind schedule. I went into work to pick up my check and was told that someone had called for me several times, but had left no clue as to who it was. Finally, I got home after a long day, not packed, nothing ready. When I walked in the door, the phone was ringing. I almost didn't answer it, but I picked it up anyway. To my surprise it was our social worker. She asked if I wanted to take our baby with us to the wedding! I really thought she was kidding.
> To make a long story short, we met with our social worker

that evening in a restaurant. We were told to pick up our baby at 1 P.M. the next day, and so we did. We took off for the wedding and made it to the rehearsal dinner. Everyone came running to see him. My dad was the first to reach us and hold our son. They announced our good news over the loudspeaker, and everyone we cared about was together to help us celebrate. It couldn't have been more perfect. The next morning, my husband and I awoke early and sat on the side of the bed and just stared in utter amazement at this little angel.

SPECIAL NEEDS

For Betty and David, who were both twenty-seven when they adopted for the first time, their desire to pursue a special needs child after having biological children was not fully understood by family and friends. Betty began, "It was especially hard for them to understand that we wished to adopt a special needs child. 'Why would you choose to take on that responsibility?' they'd ask." The couple openly discussed the circumstances surrounding the adoption of their two children, each born with Down's Syndrome, and the surprise event that occurred in between them. She also described how an open adoption situation works for them.

The mother of our first daughter was considering placing our daughter up for adoption, and wanted to speak with several prospective families. Within a few days we met and talked. Soon after, she phoned to say that she had chosen us as the adoptive family. There are no words to describe the emotion we felt. The next week or so was a whirlwind of excitement and preparation. Our study was approved and we finalized the adoption plans with the birth mother. We agreed to total openness, allowing the exchange of all identifying information, promising to send photos and letters and giving the birth family permission to visit our home occasionally. On a prearranged day and time, the birth mom and dad brought the baby (eight weeks old) to our home. I had always been afraid of meeting the birth parents and of having any contact with them, especially once the child was placed. But I was able to put those fears aside after meeting Stacy and getting to know her. Five years have gone by and I have learned so much from her. She has made me aware of the birth parent side of adoption; of the feelings and concerns they have, of the pain they feel, the guilt and remorse. I saw how she grieved and mourned for her child. It didn't happen overnight, but we have developed a close relationship. Sometimes when she doesn't call or come around for a while, I find myself missing her.

Our second adoption came about in much the same way as our first. We were informed of a baby boy, born with Down's Syndrome and a heart defect. Were we interested? Yes! Within weeks we were traveling six hours to meet the birth mom and to bring him home with us. This time I was more than willing for any amount of openness with the birth family. In fact, I actually wanted it. It's been close to two years since then, and the birth mom writes occasionally. I send photos and let her know how our son is doing. Her mother and grandmother have visited us twice. Our son's biological mother doesn't feel up to that yet but says she might one day. She knows that she's always welcome.

Our son lived with a very special foster family until he was placed with us. They were completely devoted to him for the first four months of his life. When it was confirmed that he would need surgery to repair his heart defect, Catholic Social Services decided to have him baptized. His foster mom and dad arranged the ceremony and stood in as his godparents. They videotaped the service and have since sent it to us. They were wonderful about making us feel a part of everything going on with him, even though we were hundreds of miles away. When he was just two months old, our son had open heart surgery and spent several days in intensive care, then ten more days in the hospital recovering.

Betty's fear prior to their first adoption was that they wouldn't be approved, or that their judge would deny the petition. This became an ever greater fear when soon after the placement of their daughter, she discovered (much to everyone's surprise) that she was pregnant. Three weeks before their adopted daughter's first birthday, she gave birth to a boy. The two children have been inseparable ever since and are so close in size and development, that people often ask Betty if they're twins. "We are open to the possibility of adopting a child of another race," she adds. Her advice for those considering domestic adoption is to be open to the possibility of adopting an older child, one of a different race, or one that may have special needs.

FERTILITY SPECIALISTS AND CLINICS

"Fertility specialists and clinics." The words alone can raise the hair on the back of my neck. Considering the statistics, it's not surprising that some couples play the odds. In vitro fertilizations, in which eggs and sperm are united in a laboratory dish and then transferred to the uterus, have about an 18 percent success rate. Gamete Intrafallopian Tube Transfer (GIFT), in which eggs and sperm are injected into one fallopian tube, has a success rate of 20 percent. Zygote Intrafallopian Transfer Procedure (ZIFT), sometimes considered the best treatment for low sperm counts and sluggish sperm, has a success rate of 24 percent. Intrauterine inseminations, in which sperm is injected directly into the uterus, has a success rate of only 10 percent.[1]

Many couples undergo several procedures before calling it quits. For single women and for women whose mates have low sperm counts, sperm donation can offer an option. Prospective recipients should make sure that the donor has been screened for HIV and check with their state to make sure it mandates the testing. Regulations vary. When choosing a fertility clinic, make sure it's one that's recognized by the American Society for Reproductive Medicine. Investigate its success rates and be sure and talk to other patients who have completed the clinic's programs.

FIRST THEY WERE FOSTER PARENTS

The foster-care system offered Earl and Shelly their route to adoption. To them, adopting was a gift. They grew up surrounded by foster children, as well as biological children. Initially, when they decided to adopt two large sibling groups that were available through the foster-care system, extended family members gave them little support. Over the years, Shelly remembers many difficult times—instances of favored children, prejudices and criticism.

In total, they've adopted nine children—two sibling groups of four, then one single adoption. Their first adoption, almost eleven years ago, brought them two boys and two girls. She recalled, "We were sitting at the supper table with our four children, ages three, four, five, and seven, and our youngest birth child, thirteen. I looked across the table and felt panic. These were our children forever! Can I do this?" I asked Shelly and her husband if they had met any of the children's biological parents. For some of her children, the answer was yes, though the visits were bittersweet. During these meetings, she learned that some of her children had endured some form of abuse. With maturity and a lot of hard work, she has learned to overcome some of her anger.

BIOLOGICAL PARENTS REAPPEARED

Demonstrating what can happen in the course of a domestic adoption, the following story illustrates the uncertainties of a biological mother and the circumstances that took an eleven-week-old baby girl from Katherine and her husband, Don. It's also a story of the unyielding human spirit. Even after their loss, the adoptive parents look back upon the events with a resigned optimism. Katherine observes that with the help of her supportive husband, she was able to get over the devastating event and move on.

We were matched with a couple who were getting a divorce. The wife was pregnant with their fourth child. The financial situation was not good, and she did not feel that she could raise and care for four kids alone. He is in the military. Also, they had a little girl just sixteen months older than the expected baby. They picked us to raise their new baby, partially because we're both black, and they insisted upon two black adoptive parents like they were. We developed a wonderful relationship with the birth mother, and we had met the other kids. They were healthy, beautiful children. I would have taken all four. The biological father never wanted to meet us. He said that it would be too hard on him.

One month later a healthy baby girl was born. We named her Sky and that is the name that was put on her original birth certificate. She was born by C-section and she and the birth mother were released three days later. We took our baby home. I kept in touch with the birth mom. For the first week she was upset and grieving. One thing that helped her was being able to call and say, "Hi" and ask how everything was. Since she received pictures and talked to us, she knew she had done the right thing. When Sky was born, I took two weeks off and my husband, Don, took the next two weeks. We were given four separate baby showers and had a wonderful time putting together the nursery in the theme of Peter Rabbit. As I am a teacher, I also had the whole summer off to spend with my baby.

Near the end of July, Sky and I went to Los Angeles to visit some relatives. When we got home, my husband was there. It was too early for him to be home. I decided he must have been fired. He told me that the attorney had called him and informed him that the birth parents were taking Sky back. In California, where we live, the birth parents (both if married, otherwise only the mom) have ninety days to revoke the adoption. It was just like a death. I sat down and started crying. I also asked him to please be fired instead. There was a message on our answering machine from the biological mother. I called her back and asked, "Why?" and started crying.

She was crying too, and said she couldn't talk right then. I called her the next day and Don and I spent a couple of hours trying to change her mind about getting back together with her husband, for the best interest of all her kids. She believed it was best for Sky to stay with us, as they had all they could handle and afford with the other three children. But her husband was unsure.

That afternoon we started calling relatives to tell them we were losing our daughter. Everyone was so supportive. We handed her over at 7:48 P.M. at the attorney's office. Her birth father stayed in the car. If I were to do it again, I'd make him get out and come face us. I just started screaming as they walked out of the office. If Don hadn't held me back, I would have grabbed my child back. That night an adoptive mother who had lost her son eight years ago, called and talked to us. I was so grateful to her for talking to us about the pain of this type of loss. Since then, I have let the social workers and facilitators know that we were willing to speak with any adoptive parents who might need us.

Katherine feels fortunate in being able to maintain a relationship with the biological mother. She has learned that Sky is still the child's name and she and her husband are planning to continue staying in touch with Sky's biological mother. Despite what has happened, she considers herself lucky, lucky in knowing that the child is being cared for by adults rather than young adolescents. She has also learned that Sky's birth parents are back together. "It's nice to know some good came out of this. Time is the only healer." They have more recently adopted a baby boy seven weeks of age. This time, all of his birth parent's rights have been terminated. "We used an agency instead of an attorney," Katherine added, "and it only took a few days."

Another couple discussed the failed placements that affected their lives before eventually adopting their two sons. It took them nine months to get their first son. During that waiting period they had three cases fall through. "With the first one, I spent months talking to the birth mom on the phone," explained Dawn. "We really had great conversations. But toward the end, we found out that she was going to keep the baby." Then they heard about another mother who had already given birth, but the next day she also decided to keep her baby. "Then we got hooked up with our third case. Our attorney asked if we wanted to switch cases, that they had a birth mom due any day. What they didn't tell us at the time was they were getting rid of the case we originally had, because the birth mom was receiving money from more than one couple at a time." Eventually, a three-day-old boy was placed in their home.

Their second adoption followed a year and a half later without mishap. She explained for me the regulations and intricacies regarding the finalizations of their two adoptions.

We adopted from two different states. Our first son, Charlie, came from Texas, and our second son from New York. We live in New York. At the time of our adoption, in New York a biological mom had forty-five days to change her mind unless she did a court surrender. Our son's birth mom went to court about a week after he was born; after that she couldn't change her mind, though we're still waiting to finalize his adoption. New York has two six-month periods—one, the child has to have been in your house for six months, and the other, paperwork has to be in the courts for six months. New York is a little mixed up, as they have no set rules for finalization or what to do about unknown birth fathers. It depends on the county and the judge. The judge can decide to let the two six-month periods run at the same time or back to back. Our judge said ours could run at the same time, but now that the six month waiting period is over he has no time to look at the paperwork and set a date. This part is driving me up a wall. We have no idea when we're going to finalize. With our other son from Texas, we had a date set a month after he was with us.

After hearing these stories, I found myself reflecting upon a question that I asked throughout my research: have you ever been called a hero? The overwhelming response was a loud 'No.' One man said, "We're not saints or heroes, nor are our children. We adopted because we did what we felt in our hearts was right."

---

[1] Marlene Targ Brill, Erol Amon, M.D., *Infertility and You*, Budlong Press Company, 1991, p. 41.

CHAPTER 8

Single Parenting Stories

THERE'S A CHILD
—Marla, a single adoptive parent

There's a child just beyond your reach
there's a child who has forgotten
or has never known
the warmth of a good night kiss

A child who rarely hears good job or
I love you
A child who cries in pain
due to the absence of warmth, compassion
and a place called home

There's a child
who never learned to sing nursery
rhymes with her mother or
to dance on the shoe tops of her father
or to play basketball with his uncle

There's a child who never
had the security of a safe place—

for they were raped, beaten or neglected
to the point of desperation

There's a child
who feels as though they have a
space in the center of their soul
that is like a black hole

A child who feels unworthy, lost,
alone, useless, hopeless, because
no one is there to simply say,
you shall be mine

There are children
waiting for you and they are
within your reach

WHETHER SINGLE THROUGH DIVORCE, LOSS, OR BY CHOICE, SINGLE
individuals are offered by adoption a wonderful way to become parents. It can make having children a possibility when the biological
opportunity doesn't exist. For some, pursuing a career has taken priority, so starting a family comes after their careers are well established,
too late, in some cases, to start a biological family. Others, whether
divorced or never married, want the ability to create their families
without having to wait for the right man or woman to come along.
Every situation is different and presents different opportunities.

No matter how it comes about, however, single parenting can be a
challenge with added pressures. In the best of circumstances, single
parents receive help from family members or friends, and have a good
work situation that allows enough time for the parent to devote attention to both work and home life. As a result, it may be more difficult,
if not impossible, for singles to adopt domestically. The international
adoption program for many countries, however, is open to singles and
readily accepts their applications. China, El Salvador, India, Bolivia and
Peru are some of the countries accepting single individuals, though the
legal requirements vary with each country. In addition, the volatile

nature of the governments in some of these countries, makes it difficult to know with certainty what their adoption policies will be over an extended period of time.

The National Adoption Clearing House, a federally funded organization, offers helpful information to singles and couples alike pertaining to all aspects of domestic and international adoption. They recommend that singles consider intercountry adoption. Additionally, the director of Single Parents Adopting Children Everywhere (SPACE), a Massachusetts support group, thinks that singles should consider adopting siblings. "If you want more than one child, and you want both children from the same country, you may want to adopt them at the same time" the director advises. In doing this, you will not have to deal with the very changeable international adoption scene, where a country may accept single adopters one year and close their doors the next year. It may also speed the process, since countries are eager to keep families intact and will act more expeditiously to let you adopt. The Committee for Single Adoptive Parents can provide a listing of adoption agencies that will work with singles to locate a foreign child or children.

LOCATING A CHILD THROUGH THE INTERNET

For Leanne, a successful dean of students with her local community college, attention to her career postponed parenthood until she was in her early forties. She needed to be at a point where she felt content enough with her job and position that she wouldn't view something or someone as getting in the way of furthering her career opportunities. She assumed in her twenties that she would go to college, get married and have children. Instead, her life took a much different turn. Marriage never did become a reality. Only recently has she given adoption serious consideration. She was influenced by a colleague who was pursuing her own adoption and by a visit to China during the United Nations Conference on Women. When it came time to more seriously consider adopting as a part of her life, she consulted the internet.

Once she was familiar with searching for a web site, she quickly found the best source for the information she wanted by subscribing to one of dozens of adoption news groups. She explained how important a resource it was for someone in her situation.

On a business trip, I came upon an article on adoption. I saved the article and one night I decided to check out the web sites listed at the end of it. I was able to locate a web site that listed children from foreign countries who were waiting to be adopted. The list was quite substantial. I began reviewing the children listed in China. Somehow, I just didn't feel the connection that I needed to make the next move. But I continued to check out the web site. I think that this was due to two factors. One, I really didn't think that I wanted a baby. I was really more interested in an older child, preferably a child two to three. Secondly, the names of the babies were so 'foreign' that I found myself just kind of picking at random.

On one visit to the site, I looked beyond China, specifically in the Russian and Eastern European areas. This is where I realized that I felt more comfortable. I selected three children, and e-mailed each agency involved for more information. Looking back, I then took a gigantic risk by selecting an agency right away. I'm not suggesting that I felt rushed by the agency in any way...but I really fell in love with Georgie, a little girl the agency had up for adoption, and felt this connection. Immediately after I made the commitment, I contacted regulating agencies in California to get information about the agency, Life Adoption. It would have been preferable to do this up front, but I didn't find any 'skeletons' through my inquiries, to my great relief.

The relationship between potential adoptive parents and their chosen agency is an interesting one. For most people, the process is new, so you don't have a standard of what this relationship should be like. In addition, I've been reading some of the postings on the adoption news groups. People talk about the quality of their relationship with their agency, but you don't really know what that means. For example, one parent may consider one call a month sufficient, and assume that when there is news, it will be forwarded. Another might consider this same thing neglect. On the other hand, it seems to me that proper use of e-mail could really be an answer to this dilemma.

Leanne described how she selected her daughter. "Honestly, I selected Georgie because she was born the day before my mother's birthday." Leanne also said that seeing Georgie's picture on the internet made her heart skip a beat. "Somehow I now believe that God was just keeping this little one for me." The agency e-mailed her the next day. Within a few days, she was sent a video tape and medical information on the little girl. Her soon-to-be-adopted daughter would continue living in an orphanage in Botosani, Romania, a farming area in the northeast section of the country, until the adoption was made final. "I couldn't have imagined losing her and then immediately thinking about shifting gears and considering another child. I would have needed time to get over it, if that had happened."

Now that her daughter is here, Leanne plans to take advantage of the preschool and after-school care her campus offers. Another plus for Leanne, because her college is very "family friendly," and she plans on taking a sabbatical, so that her first months of single motherhood will allow her to be at home.

OH, BOY! THREE BOYS!

To Gretchen, three Latin American countries offered different routes to building her family. Not once, not twice, but three times, she journeyed off to unfamiliar foreign countries fueled by desire and love. She adopted three sons: Edward, who was born in Honduras; Larry, born in Paraguay; and Henry, born in Colombia. In addition to raising her three sons single-handedly, Gretchen is editor of Buenas Noticias, the newsletter for the Latin American Parent Association (LAPA), a nonprofit organization in the state of Maryland. LAPA is not an adoption agency, but rather a volunteer association of adoptive parents. She said parenting three boys alone is not an easy task, but one that she wouldn't trade for the world.

Her second adoption required a trip to Paraguay to pick up her son, Larry. It was a trip filled with frustration resulting from logistical nightmares and a missing visa photo, along with the normal stress anyone typically experiences visiting an unfamiliar country. As a result of her experiences, she recommends Colombia to individuals who may be undecided about what country to pursue, though the travel requirements are rather long and complicated.[1]

On my second adoption, when I returned to Asuncion, in Paraguay, I met many adoptive parents who had simply remained in Paraguay rather than making two trips. Unfortunately for them, the long delay had translated into logistical nightmares. My agency had told me up front that it didn't help to speed up the case to remain in the country and encouraged me to return home after my court appearance. I'm glad I did. Most of the people I met had been in Asuncion for an average of seven weeks—and were still not finished. One single woman had been stranded for nine weeks; another, for eleven. Many complained about uncommunicative lawyers and unhelpful facilitators or agencies.

Although I arrived on a Monday, my visa interview at the embassy wasn't until Thursday, due to the backlog of parents waiting in Asuncion. (On a side note, I would highly recommend staying at The Excelsior, both for its affordability and its space.) When it came time for the interview, it went smoothly, except for the missing visa pictures. Déjà vu, I thought, as the exact thing happened when processing Edward's visa in Honduras. Eventually, my escort went back to the photo studio to get new pictures made from the negatives on file. My new son, Larry and I flew home on a full airplane, traveling through Sao Paulo, Brazil, and on to Miami. Edward's initial reaction to Larry has been interesting, to say the least. Slowly, though, he's accepted the fact that Larry is here to stay.

When Gretchen felt ready to start the process again for her third adoption, she'd decided upon Columbia. After reviewing the material she'd received about the country, Gretchen needed to find an agency to do a home study update and to do the postplacement supervision required by Colombian law. There were several agencies with programs in Colombia. "I settled upon an agency that offered me a deal," she said. "I still wasn't in any great hurry—a feeling I had never experienced in my prior two adoptions. My other two sons kept me busy enough!"

Gretchen was offered a referral, went through the various coordination steps and then came up against a slight roadblock. The United States government wanted her to have her two sons naturalized before they would proceed further with the third adoption. They also imposed a rather unrealistic deadline of two weeks to get it done. Gretchen went quickly into motion by enlisting the aid of one of her state's senators. She received the forms, submitted the package in person at INS, and was successful in getting the citizenship certificates one week after applying.

She made two trips to Colombia, although during her interview with Colombian officials she was pressured to stay in the country. "I told them point blank that my new son, Henry, was perfectly content to have met me, and would be happy to return to his foster home to wait for my return. My two sons at home, on the other hand, would suffer greatly." The officials relented, although they insisted that Henry stay with Gretchen that evening and accompany her to the airport as she left the country.

Three weeks later, she was on her way back to Bogota. She had decided that her boys could not stand another separation, especially since Gretchen didn't know exactly how long she'd be away from home. "It was early December, and I hated to impose on friends and family so close to the holidays. I begged my sister to come along with me, and she finally agreed, although she had to bring her daughter along as well. What a sight we must have been going back to pick up Henry—two moms, with three children under the age of four, international travelers taking in the sights of Bogota."

One of the quirks of the Colombian adoption system was that she had to sign the adoption decree at the court before it could be released. This hadn't happened in her two previous adoptions, and it complicated matters greatly. "We traveled to the courthouse through the incredible Bogota traffic, literally hours traveling scant miles, only to find that the decree wasn't ready." After some additional waiting at one of the public notary offices, Gretchen and family emerged with the certified copies and proceeded to the next step, which was obtaining a new birth certificate for Henry.

At this point, Gretchen had to deal with a new wrinkle: the birth certificate needed to originate from Henry's place of birth. Although her son had been living in Bogota for some time, he had actually been born in a place in southern Colombia, almost in the jungle. Someone was going to have to travel there to get it. For a moment, Gretchen thought she would be the one, instead, her lawyer took on the job.

"This was on a Tuesday," she explained, "so it looked like nothing further would get accomplished until the following Monday as there was only one flight going to that part of Columbia each week.'"

Gretchen's parents had been living in Guayaquil, Ecuador, for the past five months, so while waiting for the attorney's return, she and her sister, along with their three children, went there by way of Quito. They reached Guayaquil uneventfully and spent a wonderful five days with her parents. Gretchen described what happened when she returned to Bogota.

> We waited once again, as the lawyer failed to return on Monday, nor did he call. Late Tuesday evening he finally showed up with the birth certificate. I uttered a silent, 'thank you,' and we were off. The next day, we reached the passport office and waited in yet another line, only to find that their computers were down. The next day was our embassy visit, and I was determined to talk my way into getting the visa in the morning and making the 1 P.M. flight home. Thankfully, things went smoothly at the embassy, and, also passing through immigration in Miami on our way back to the United States.

Gretchen and her sons have continued to adjust to their new situation. Talking openly about their experiences has helped the children understand their own origins a little better. "We sometimes talk about traveling to Colombia, and Edward often asks me, 'You got me in Honduras. Right, Mom?' and then Henry chimes in,' You got me in Colombia. Right, Mom?' We continue to talk about how families are built in different ways. For now, they understand simple things." Gretchen is certainly not the first and only single adoptive mother of three toddlers, but acknowledged that "trying to cram a full-time job into three days a week, has been an impossible task."

SPECIAL NEEDS, SPECIAL LOVE, SPECIAL SITUATION

Another parent, Roberta, was married when the adoption of their special needs child was completed, but became single soon after the child was in their home. Roberta's husband left after it was revealed that their long-awaited son had autism. He said, "It's either me, or the baby." She's quick to defend her ex-husband's actions. "My ex-husband is a wonderful man, he just stinks at being a father. He couldn't take it anymore. Taylor would scream and rock for hours on end. I think my husband was very embarrassed."

She tackles parenting Taylor with the same optimistic spirit she applies to her career as a social worker. After waiting seven years for her son, and then being faced with caring for a child with a major disability, Roberta feels a special type of unconditional love for Taylor and values deeply their life together. She views her life with her disabled son as an entirely different kind of parenting journey, one characterized by constant adjustment. From the start, though, she has felt spiritually connected to her son.

> After seven incredibly long years of waiting for an assignment, I cried and cried when I saw our son. When I first held him it was "coming home," as if I had known this baby all of my life. When he first opened his eyes to look at me, I remember saying, "Hi, there, I'm your mommy. I've been waiting for you all of my life. You'll never be alone again."

Roberta found out after Taylor had entered her life that his biological mother was schizophrenic. The agency didn't mention this little detail because they felt, mistakenly, that Taylor would be unaffected if he were placed with a good family. When her son was sixteen months old, however, Roberta noticed that there was something different about him. "He didn't make any eye contact," she explained, "rocked for hours in his crib, and had severe mood swings, from crying hysterically to laughing." The children's hospital in Roberta's home state told her that Taylor would never distinguish his mother from strangers, and that he would never be able to feed himself. They recommended she put him away before she became more attached. She continued:

> When I became a mother, I made that choice with no conditions or barriers. That's the type of love Taylor and I share— unconditional love. Many people don't ever get to experience that. I may not have gotten the path I wished I had in regards to the baseball games, gymnastics, getting to be a grandmother. Instead, I got a path that led me into an entirely different

kind of parenting journey. I never take for granted hearing that word mommy, as it is the only word Taylor can say. I'm fortunate that I also do social work in the field of disabilities, so I apply many things learned at work, at home. When I tell the families that I work with, "I understand," they realize I'm not just another professional who says they understand.

Today, her son is thirteen, and able to feed himself and walk unassisted, although he takes up to one hundred baths a day and can be very aggressive. Roberta is dealing with her son's challenging behavior the only way she can, on a daily basis. She also fights battles with the special education program Taylor attends. She's on the governor's planning council for people with disabilities, on the boards of many human rights groups, and seeks out virtually every parent support group she can find. "There's literally not a day that goes by when I'm not having to argue with someone for my son's rights. He has the right to be treated with respect and dignity, and to have an education."

Against All Odds

This next story involves a single African American woman named Cassandra. It demonstrates what a person with determination and perseverance can do, even in the face of adversity. Although she adopted an infant nine years ago, her state's Social Services Department initially said that it would be practically impossible for her as a single woman to adopt a healthy infant.

Since Cassandra was thirty-five at the time, people thought she was crazy for pursuing her wish. After turning down a child whose parents were drug users, she was alerted one day that a three-week-old girl was up for adoption. Cassandra believes matters moved so quickly because she demanded her home-study form back from her original agency in order to circulate it to others. It worked.

People asked if I was crazy. But I didn't let that stop me. I had one agency tell me that I would never be given an infant. 'HA! HA! HA!' I said to them nine months later, with my baby girl in my arms, no thanks to them. Eventually, I connected with an adoption advocate coalition on adoptable children. They put me in touch with Catholic Home Bureau, (CHB) in Manhattan. A decent group of people, although they gave me some grief in the beginning. At the time, I was only the second single person they had dealt with, but eleven months later I became the mom of the most beautiful baby girl in the world!

Here's what happened in a nutshell. On lunchtime, with my sister in tow, I went to see the baby at the foster mom's house. I held her, cried and cried, put her back in her foster mother's arms and told the CHB Director that I would pick her up at the end of the week. HA! They said, 'You'll take her today.' My sister left her job, then went to tell her family and get her car. I went back to work, told my supervisor, left work, went to CHB and picked up my baby. There was no adoption fee, though they did ask for the cost of the birth mom's stay at CHB's Unwed Mother's Home, a cost of about $5,000. I told them I was broke. They accepted my thanks and I left. I eventually paid the lawyer $550 for the court proceedings.

Cassandra had been working for a company whose policy viewed adoption leave of absences differently from biological maternity leaves. She was allowed to take eight weeks off from work, the same amount of time offered to biological mothers working for corporations with over five hundred employees—with one major difference: hers was unpaid leave. She was able, however, to take advantage of a federal law passed in 1993 granting health insurance coverage for adopted children. This provision guarantees that adopted children, from the time of their placement, are allowed the same access to health insurance as biological children, regardless of preexisting conditions.

I asked Cassandra if her daughter had experienced any hostility about being adopted. She expressed her concerns over two incidents that indicate what adopted children and their parents may face.

During this past school year, a neighbor's little girl stood up on the bus and announced to twenty kids that my daughter was adopted. She told me that it didn't bother her until the little girl said my daughter was adopted because her real mother didn't want her. Of course, she was totally devastated by that, and it took me a couple of weeks to get her back together about being adopted. This 'little darling's' mom had driven my daughter to school in the morning every day since preschool. But after that experience, we parted company, and I put my daughter on a private van. The second incident involves a cousin. He told my daughter that she wasn't really his cousin because she was adopted. Her reply to him was, 'My mom picked me. Your mom had no choice—I'm the special one.'

Nine Times The Fun

Women like Gretchen, with her three South American sons, and like Sydney, with her nine children from around the world, adopting more than one child was essential. Sydney's nine multicultural children came to be their own much-needed support group in what Sydney described as a racist society here in America. She believes that if there was a list of socially endangered species in the modern age, large families would rank right up there with the polar bear, the mountain gorilla, and the spotted newt. She adopted over twenty years ago, when the possibilities for adopting as a single were practically nonexistent. At the time, she was teaching and had to stretch her income to the breaking point to cover her growing family. She explained her experiences and offered her opinion about adoption.

The joys of a large family have far outweighed the burdens, even on a modest income. My decision to parent so large a brood on a teacher's salary was based upon my love of children, my intense desire to be a parent, an optimistic outlook, an excellent insurance policy, and a firm belief that children— especially those adopted transracially—benefit from growing up with many brothers and sisters like them. Adoption is basically a selfish act. For me it met a very real human need to complete a life cycle that I might have missed otherwise. Adopting internationally was my only option back in the mid-seventies when few agencies were willing to become involved in domestic single parent adoptions. But, Spaulding for Children in Westfield, New Jersey, was different.

They invited me to an open meeting and agreed to work

with me. Before they could locate a child, however, I moved ahead on my own. I contacted an agency in Pennsylvania and inquired about their program in Korea. Four months later, Bob arrived. At that time, he was considered a 'hard-to-place' child because of his age (two) and the fact that he was a boy. Then when Ellie arrived, just eighteen months later, I felt torn between two same age rivals who were determined to have all of me, all at the same time. When the third and fourth followed in rapid succession (Caroline, eleven, then Charles, one), I was finally forced, out of sheer exhaustion, to reconsider my entire premise of parenting. I no longer could cherish or nourish the belief that I was Superwoman.

Over the next several years, five more youngsters, Austin, Allie, Meredith, Jessy and Abigail, journeyed thousands of miles to join those already in Sydney's home. Some braved harrowing escapes from their homelands to find refuge in America; others came with undiagnosed handicaps. All came with both tragic losses and untold gifts. Recently retiring from teaching to be a full-time, milk-and-cookies mom, Sydney was able to spend her additional time working in the field of adoption. A close friend, also an adoptive parent and a social worker, asked Sydney to help start an adoption agency. Today, Seedlings, Inc. places children from Central and South America and China with eager families just starting out on the adoption road. The rest of her time is spent publishing and editing a national adoption magazine for those already parenting. She concluded, "In life, you have a couple of choices. You can stand and be counted or you can get lost in the crowd. Our family is proud to stand and be counted!"

---

[1] Conditions affecting international adoptions are often changeable. Individuals considering adoption should consult their attorney or agency for the most reliable and up-to-date information.

CHAPTER 9

If You've Got the Faith, Do You Have the Finances?

May the favor of God always rest upon you.
　　　　　—Unknown author

A penny saved is a penny earned.
　　　　　—Often attributed to Benjamin Franklin

HAVING A RELIGIOUS AFFILIATION AND HAVING ADEQUATE FINANCIAL resources are two aspects of adoption that can't be overlooked. To varying degrees, they are requirements by many agencies, private entities, and countries. For example, adoption agencies that are associated with a particular church are going to seek out parents of that religion. That's not to say people who are not religious can't find agencies willing to work with them, but they might not be the most convenient agency or an individual's first choice. In a domestic adoption, a birth mother's religious views are often considered when placing a child. With many international adoptions, prospective adoptive individuals are required to detail in their home study their plans for integrating religion into their newly adopted child's or children's lives.

In Guatemala, for example, such a religious requirement is strictly enforced. We had to have a letter from our pastor giving testimony to our moral character and to our intent to raise our child within an organized religion. Although my husband and I had attended church regularly as children (he as a Catholic, I as a Methodist), we had no affiliation with a particular church as a married couple. So, in addition to juggling two careers, applying for passports and reviewing paperwork with our attorney, we had to become acquainted with, attend and select a church, then ask its pastor for help.

The church we chose is literally, as the song says, "a little brown church in the vale." It's a tiny place, sitting tucked away on a knoll in a small valley in an almost forgotten town. Its congregation is lucky to total 100 on Christmas and Easter. The remainder of the year, more often than not, a stubbornly caring and conscientious group of thirty or forty hearty souls occupies the pews, reads from the Book and prays for healing and redemption. It's a church that greets every new member, like my husband and myself, with an outstretched handshake or, in the case of the women, with a hug. Stepping into that church was like stepping into a broken-in pair of loafers: it felt comfortable. Its pastor, a round-faced, portly man who wore a neatly trimmed beard and a nice suit every Sunday, would, we hoped, help us become parents.

Meeting with him was much like meeting with our social worker. It was not an encounter we looked forward to, but in the end it was surprisingly supportive and productive. We attempted to demonstrate our knowledge of religion (limited as it was), our reverence for God, and our intent to raise our adopted child with an appreciation for the importance of the nonsecular part of life.

When interviewing people for this book, I was surprised at how readily so many of them acknowledged the strong role religion played in their journeys through the adoption process. The great majority of parents, in fact, said that their religious faith had been a critical factor in helping them deal with the various crises that arose on their path to parenthood: the loss of fertility; the loss of an assignment; a major delay in the adoption process, such as a legal setback; or the death of an assigned child.

One has only to read the following tribute one couple wrote to the son they never adopted to see how important God and faith were to them.

IN MEMORY OF PATRICK
June 21, 1994—Sept. 26, 1994

We never held you in our arms
but in our hearts you stayed,
a little boy, so very sick,
and every day we prayed.

Your big brown eyes stared back at us,
a photo, all we had,
but in those eyes we saw God's love,
this was a special lad.

Three months you fought for that next breath,
alas, the struggle passed,
and into Jesus's arms you went,
strength and peace at last.

We asked the Lord to send you home,
to our place, we assumed,
but in his mercy and his grace,
he made that special room.

And though our hearts still ache for you
and tears they still do flow,
we know our God has chosen you
and he will watch you grow.

So Patrick, this is our good-bye
to our babe, our boy so fine,
we know one day we'll hold you close
but that's in God's own time.

Praying for Snow, Aunt Eleonore, and a Healthy Son

Parents commonly relied on prayer as a coping mechanism. I know I did. In fact, I prayed often during the course of adopting our son. Perhaps because I was used to asking God for all sorts of things as a child: for lots of snow, for a day off from school, for my pet guinea pig to get well, for my Aunt Eleonore to somehow move back home from faraway places, and for hundreds of kid's things, now lost in oblivion. As an adult, I had prayed for the right partner, and a happy marriage. And I'd prayed, too, for a family. So when it came to adoption, asking God for a healthy son came easy. In the end, I came to need prayer like I needed to eat, because some things in life were simply too complex to grasp without it. What I didn't understand for a long time was the type of family God wanted me to have.

Some parents specifically cited Biblical verses as testament to their beliefs. Diane, the wife in one couple that had gone through an international adoption, said, "God promises to give children to the childless wife, so that she becomes a happy mother (Psalm 113: 8), and I can see now that for us, adoption may be the fulfillment of that promise."

Others simply attributed their fortune—good or bad—to God. "It was meant to be," more than one parent said, and "God heard our prayers" was repeated over and over. For Helen from Michigan, it was God's decision that she would not be able to bear children, and she accepted her fate as His will. Another mom felt that God was punishing her for some reason by making her unable to conceive. Most parents, however, felt that God was merciful and was leading them onward. One mother said she felt the Holy Spirit working within her throughout the course of their Russian adoption. It was God, ultimately, that would give these people the strength to work through whatever difficulties they encountered, not their spouses or their neighbors. Through God, they felt blessed with their adoptive child or children. "God has given me the desires of my heart," said one adoptive dad.

Often people reached out to their parishes, churches, and synagogues, for support, camaraderie and advice. One adoptive mother said that a friend from their church fellowship offered the support they so badly needed. "We must acknowledge our friend, Joe, who really started us on the current path to adoption," she told me. "At Saturday morning prayer meetings my husband, would share with Joe the emotional burden of wanting children but not being able to have any. One day, Joe gave my husband an article that had appeared in a Baptist newsletter about infertile couples. It inspired us to seek other infertile couples for fellowship." With further help from their pastor, Jerry and his wife located a nearby group and began attending meetings.

Among the adoptive parents I interviewed, some were practicing Christians; others were simply living the kind of life they felt Christ wanted them to live; others were members of the Jewish faith; others followed Hinduism; and some, though they considered themselves spiritual, did not follow any specific organized religion.

One mom who adopted from India belongs to the Baha'I faith, a religion that teaches that all religions come from the same source and that all mankind is one family. It teaches that if a person can only educate some children, it should be the daughters, so that they can go on to educate their own children in the next generation. Finally, a small group of those I interviewed didn't mention or have any religious affiliation, but found solace instead, in journal writing, meditation, and talking with people in similar situations.

Regardless of their religious or spiritual orientation, many adoptive parents felt they could "walk" through the more difficult issues with God's helping hand.

WHAT YOU NEED TO KNOW

"I don't understand," a friend of mine questioned. "Why does it cost so much to adopt a child?" At the time, I wasn't able to give her a thorough explanation. We had just begun to think about pursuing an adoption, and, frankly, we didn't have the answers. We simply knew that it would take 'x-amount of dollars' to adopt a child from Guatemala. It wasn't until we'd almost completed our adoption and I'd read the information shared with me as I wrote this book that I could explain it to her, and tell her also of the many variables that can affect the final cost. Money—sometimes a lot of it can play a critical role in an adoption.

The basic fees can be expected to range on the low side from less than $10,000 for a domestic adoption through an agency, up to $25,000 for an "average" international adoption. Private United States adoptions can occasionally run as high as $60,000. Of course, complications of any kind can and do arise, driving the costs much higher. Corrupt attorneys, dishonest agencies and baby brokering can easily escalate the costs. One couple, who wished to remain anonymous, acknowledged paying close to $40,000 on two different occasions, to two different biological mothers who subsequently changed their minds about giving their babies up. The couple still has no baby. A red flag should wave if you've spent more than the usual amount and you have no child.

Financial options for prospective parents, however, do offer hope. For example, some agencies have sliding scales for lower-income families and others give financial breaks to adoptive parents when the adoption involves an older child or one with special needs. Some even offer payment plans. Rose felt worthless not having enough money to complete her adoption. Love should conquer all, she felt, no matter what. She summed up her feelings this way:

I FELT SO SMALL

i came forth with joy and fear.
i talked too much every time i was called by a social worker.
i called the agency almost every day to share some new tidbit.
i didn't understand their ho-hum attitude.

i was so enthusiastic that i was bursting at the seams.
i told my coworkers, family and all my friends
that i was going to adopt and finally have my own daughter.

it took one month to get my first call.
it was almost two months before i got invited to a meeting.
i had problems understanding the application, though i did
get help from a friend.

after my first visit,
i felt so small because i was told

"your income won't afford a child much;
a child really should have their own bedroom right away;
the appearance of your neighborhood is
barely passable; and please focus on
using better diction when you speak."

i felt so small.
i just quit.
i guess all this love and joy in my heart just wasn't enough.
i just didn't feel good enough.

The majority of the parents I heard from, like Lauren and James from Maine, described themselves as middle-class Americans, and saw the cost of adoption as their biggest hurdle. "We really had to pool our minds as well as our financial resources to make it happen." In general, these parents feel that adoption is not accessible to everyone and think that this needs to change.

With Elizabeth, Lauren and James' second adoption, they had no additional money set aside, so they were forced to take out a loan—about $8,000. Since they were repeat adopters, however, their agency gave them a 10 percent deduction. The agency's fee had increased $2,000, so total placement costs were about $10,800. As with their first adoption, the couple received a $3,500 agency reimbursement, but for some reason struggled to pay off this loan more than the previous one. "I guess it was the extra expense of having two children with double the daycare costs." The family was also in the process of building a bigger house. "We are a solid middle-class family, but we have no windfalls such as inheritances or lottery winnings."

Securing a loan also made it possible for a family from the Southwest to move ahead with their adoption plans. They approached their two adoptions by looking at them as simply two more debt obligations the family had to fulfill, like paying off a mortgage or a college loan.

Kathleen's adoption cost about $10,000. Remember, this was a very small, nonprofit agency. Nowadays, $10,000 seems like nothing. But it might as well have been $100,000, because we didn't have it. We had saved about $3,000 and simply borrowed the rest. We wrote the agency a check and hurried home to arrange for a loan. I can remember calling my credit union and describing what I wanted to do. Later, when I walked into the credit union with a six-day-old infant, everyone knew who I was. It took us quite a while to pay it off—but we did (like buying a new car). We also got an unexpected bonus, as my company reimbursed us $3,500 for our first adoption, once it was finalized. But the $3,500 was treated like regular income, so after taxes there was only $2,300 left.

Another couple said of their two domestic adoptions that nothing can come in the way of adopting when it's your heart's desire. Affording the adoption, in fact, was the least of their worries:

I guess when a person wants a child so desperately, money is no object. You think to yourself that you would pay anything to get a baby. Thankfully, we didn't have to do that. The adoption agency charged according to your income, so it was fair for everyone. When our daughter was born, my husband had a job that paid very little. I think our fee for her was about $3,500. That included everything. But when our son was born, my husband had gotten a job with the United States Post Office and I had gotten a job with the State of Iowa, both very good-paying jobs. His adoption ended up costing roughly $6,000, including attorney fees. We scrimped and saved for these two little miracles. Also my folks were very well-to-do people who helped with the finances a lot!

A New Son or A New Septic System?

"The major misconception I've found in the public at large," began Christie, "is the idea that since these children were abandoned, their adoptions must have been more or less free." Christie and Jim, her husband, who have adopted several children from India, say that some people are dumbfounded to hear that they paid over $10,000 to adopt each child.

Most people can't understand why adoption should cost anything at all. (And our Indian adoptions were cheap by most standards). A few people exclaim, "They're so cute! How could their mothers have given them away?" Of course, it burns me up when they say this in front of my kids (not to mention my favorite question, "How much did you pay for them?"). There seem to be a lot of people in the world who are curious, but ham-handed, when it comes to asking their very natural questions about our family.

The couple's first adoption was paid out of savings amassed during the previous years. Their second adoption was financed by selling a house that was larger than they needed and moving into one that was substantially smaller. Their third adoption was financed by what Christie termed "creative budgeting," and by an increase in the amount they saved during the intervening years. She admitted that they still drive the same cars they drove when they were first married thirteen years ago. "And we've lived for three years with a 'crapped out' (no pun intended) septic system, so that we could spend the money we had on adopting our third child. Using a porta-potty whenever it rains is no fun, but what choice did we have when the options were a son or a new septic system?" Though they don't have savings for retirement and have nothing set aside for their children's educations, they do have a decent joint income and an attitude of letting the future take care of itself.

ARM YOURSELF WITH KNOWLEDGE AND OPTIONS

A licensed social worker shared his expertise about the financial aspect of domestic adoptions. He noted that fees, like many other elements of adoption, are subject to change.

At the last agency I worked for, the average cost to the agency was about $13,400. This cost includes maternity counseling costs for the more than 80 percent of maternity clients who do not follow adoption plans for their child. The average cost to the adopting family was about $12,000. The exact fee for a placement without special needs was determined by a sliding fee based on the formula of $7,500, plus 10 percent of the family's average annual income for the past two years up, to a maximum fee of $17,500. This fee covered application, seminar, home studies, maternity counseling, adoption preparation, preplacement, delivery medical expenses, any birth mother's living expenses falling within agency guidelines, all legal expenses related to the termination of parental rights, agency overhead and agency public relations expenses. If at all possible, I strongly recommend that a family find an agency with an adoption fee that will not have what is called "pass through" expenses added to it for medical, living, and legal expenses related to maternity. Those expenses should be included in the one adoption fee. There are agencies that do not agree with this position.

He estimated that with most agencies handling an open adoption, half of the money goes to staff costs; 5 to 10 percent goes toward legal expenses; 15 percent for office and supplies; 20 to 25 percent for birth mother expenses and 5 to 10 percent for public relations expenses. This distribution, he said, will vary widely from agency to agency. He also offered some advice about checking the credentials of an agency before doing business with it.

Just as you get in touch with the licensing division in your state to check out one part of the professional record of an agency before you sign on with it, you should also call the local Better Business Bureau to check on its financial history. You must have the business phone number for the company you want to check up on. Hopefully, it will be listed. Just because the founder of an agency has written a book about adoption, do not assume that the agency is in good standing. Several years ago, such an agency in the Southwest went bankrupt, leaving in the lurch 170 adoptive families who had paid fees but had not yet received placements.

Another possible option for finding ways to lower the cost of adopting is to shop around—shop agencies, shop attorneys, and shop countries. With international adoption, some countries fees are lower than others. As an example, the fee with one agency for adopting from Honduras is $11,000, which includes all translations of documents, legal expenses and services, initial medical evaluation, lab tests and up to three months of foster care. Chinese adoptions, sometimes referred to as "the easiest in the world," have been running about $8,500.

For domestic adoptions involving children with special needs, financial help is available through both the Federal title IV-E Program under the Social Security Act and various state programs. Each state's program is different, so it's important for families who are interested in obtaining adoption subsidies to contact their local department of social services to determine what is available in their state. Each state agency, for example, has its own definition of "special needs" to use in identifying children eligible for adoption subsidies. Generally, a child's special needs relate to age (an older child), membership in a minority group, a medical condition, siblings (brothers and sisters who should not be separated), or handicaps (a child with a physical, emotional or mental disability). The financial assistance program is also open to foster parents who may already have established an emotional bond with a special-needs child in need of a permanent home.

Under both federal and state programs, adoptive parents of a child with special needs are eligible for a one-time payment of nonrecurring adoption expenses incurred in connection with the adoption. These expenses include the fees of adoption, court costs, attorney fees and other expenses directly related to the legal adoption.

To further ease the financial blow, many states offer tax credits to individuals like Lauren and James. In addition, more and more companies on a national level are offering tax incentives for adoptive parents. Even military families, who traditionally have had a difficult time adopting, are entitled to benefits of up to $2,000 a year for reasonable and necessary expenses associated with adoptions finalized after October 1, 1990. Previously, military families have been hindered by rules and criteria such as lengthy residency requirements, mandatory meetings that conflict with military schedules, and home ownership. Now the military benefits cover public and private adoption fees charged by an agency in a foreign country; placement fees, legal fees, medical and hospital expenses of a newborn; and medical expenses incurred by a birth mother.

In the end, sliding fee or no sliding fee, assistance or no assistance, tax credit or no tax credit, loan or no loan, for many people, a price simply can't be put upon the opportunity to become a parent. "If there's a will, there's a way," is a belief held by many adopting individuals when they assess their financial situation. Christie summed up her feelings this way: "I imagine we'll both be working into our seventies, and that the kids will end up working their way through college or trade school. But we all have each other and that's what's important."

Chapter 10

For the Sake of Tradition

FAMILY TRADITIONS BRIGHTEN THE SUM OF OUR EXPERIENCES. SOME traditions are performed nightly, others take place around the holidays, still others are celebrated annually or once every five or ten years. Some are simple, some are ornately complex. That's partly their beauty. Traditions can follow many patterns and can be the connective tissue between generations, experiences and cultures. Often, the most cherished ones have their roots in childhood. Parenting is a good avenue both for reviving old family traditions and for creating new ones.

A GOOD PIE AND A GOOD SLED

Picking cherries from a backyard tree and then pitting the tiny treasures to turn them into a scrumptious pie is a cherished family tradition from my childhood. It's as indelibly etched into my mind as jumping over sidewalk cracks as a young girl to avoid breaking my mother's back. Back then, and I suppose even now, squirrels and bluejays seemed to be everywhere in my midwestern hometown, and squirrels and bluejays loved our cherry tree. My family tried all sorts of inventions to scare the robbing pests away from our prized fruit. One year, we hung aluminum pie tins on long strings from all the branches. "When the wind blows, it'll scare 'em away," we told our neighbors.

Another time, we wrapped a thick black rubber hose around the base of the tree. That was to look like a snake. Another season, Dad borrowed my brother's slingshot and spent most evenings after work firing rocks out from the kitchen window instead of mowing the lawn. Sadly, though we picked cherries almost every year, most seasons we didn't net enough of the little jewels to fill the pie shell. In eight seasons, we enjoyed only three homemade cherry pies with my mother's homemade latticed top.

Going sledding was another big family event. After every snowfall over four inches, we happily pulled our sleds and saucers from their tucked-away places in our garage. Winter after winter, sledding was an exciting and much-anticipated ritual. Part of the fun for me was sledding with my older brother. He carried the stub of a burned candle in his coat pocket and he'd rub it on the partly rusted steel runners of our red Flexible Flyer to make it go faster. Some years our parents would come along. One year, my mother twisted an ankle. Another year, dad suffered quite a nasty bruise and had a hole sliced in his nicest leather jacket when a runaway sled careened over his arm. For awhile it looked as though we would be building a tradition of injury.

I learned, through years of sledding, that in order to get the best runs it depended on knowing exactly when to hit the slopes. Timing was everything. If we were one of the first to arrive, the Flexible Flyer would absolutely die in its tracks. And, of course, if we arrived at the site too late, the best and faster routes had already turned into rutted, worn patches with pieces of grass stubbornly poking through. So, we tried to arrive sometime in the middle of the day, when the snow was packed down and slickened by the kids who did the hard work of breaking it in for us. Every good run required a push from the top by somebody you trusted. Sometimes I did crash into a tree and ended the day, dragging my smashed sled behind me like a tail between my legs. Of course, after every exhilarating trip down the hill, a person had to make the awful trip back up. Sledding taught a lesson more valuable than learning the monotonous details of the Battle of Gettysburg or the intricate logarithms behind trigonometry. It taught me to accept the good with the bad. So we are most eagerly looking forward to helping our son, Michael, steer away from the trees and pick enough cherries for a pie.

How Important Are Family Rituals to You and Your Family?

Many parents and waiting parents acknowledged the importance of these family rituals. Abbey, an adoptive mom living in Boulder, Colorado, with her husband, Mark, and their two children, has fond memories of two of her favorite family rituals built around food and the Christmas holiday.

Traditions are very important, because they help us connect with our older generations. I think that's why newly married couples often experience conflict around birthdays, Christmas, and other holidays, because each person's traditions are usually quite different. One of the most meaningful traditions for me focuses on food, as it is an intensely emotional part of life. Mark and I enjoy dinner together as a family at least five time a week, and did so more often when our children were small. When it comes to holidays, food makes the day special. I revel in our Christmas traditions and look forward to passing these on to our children. Food was always given as gifts for family and friends, and over Christmas Eve dinner is still a creative, nontraditional feast like those I enjoyed growing up. Afterward, our family always went to a beautiful Episcopalian church on the river for the midnight mass.

Reading to kids topped the list of many people's favorite rituals, including Bonnie's and her husband, Jim's. When their children are old enough to understand, they plan on continuing the bedtime story ritual that each of them grew up with. Bonnie's parents have kept many of the books she owned as a child, so she'll be able to share these same books and stories with her children. Traveling is another important part of family life for Bonnie. Her parents took a two-week trip across America when she was a young girl, and the couple would love to continue this tradition so that their children can see the country the way she had.

Daily rituals often involve bedtime or revolve around mealtime. "Once our two kids went into bed," said another mom Julie, "I would sit on the bedside and read them a story, say prayers, and sing "Amazing Grace." Julie and her husband have also carried on a tradition from her youth by occasionally creating a family 'holiday.' A sudden decision is made that no one goes into work or school that day. "Instead, we play hooky and spend the day enjoying being together by going on a family outing. It really gives us a sense of togetherness." Another family with three children holds hands around the table and says grace one by one.

> If we change the routine, our daughter corrects us. Even the baby joins in and says a loud 'Amen' when we're finished. Bedtime is a favorite ritual. It consists of three hugs, three kisses and a song. Then we blow kisses as I leave the room. In the mornings, each child comes into my room, snuggles for a few minutes and then gets ready for school, even my 15-year-old daughter! We also just started a ritual where my two daughters each choose a part of the meal for that particular night. Then we go around the table and say one good thing about each girl being part of our family. It was interesting because my youngest boy (ten), who has had the hardest time adjusting to his new position in the family, said, 'I'm glad that my younger sister made me a big brother, and that Patricia smiles at me when I play peekaboo.'

The act of adopting can open the door to many new rituals. Parents can acknowledge some of the most important days in the lives of their adopted children—occasions like "gotcha day" or "remembrance day," when the new parent or parents first held their adopted child. Days like "naturalization day," when internationally adopted children become United States citizens, are natural beginnings for the establishment of a new family tradition. So are days that are set aside to recognize the festivals and holidays from the birth country of an internationally adopted child. Choosing a special day to remember the birthdays of an adopted child's birth parents can also be a way to a new tradition in a family's life. Knowing the exact date of such birthdays, however, can be next to impossible. Consequently, some families celebrate the remembrance day of the birth parents on the anniversary of their child's birth. David and Celeste's family, for example, built a routine around their prayers of thanks on that day: "Dear God, thank you so much for bringing our child into our lives. Please watch over her birth family, keep them healthy and happy, and find a way to let them know what a wonderful child they have given us. Amen."

Singles and couples who have adopted internationally can make their child's birth nationality an opportunity to celebrate multicultural events. Most parents feel that integrating customs is important, but some leave it up to the children to decide if, how, and when to do it. In some instances, the children have felt that immersing themselves in their native cultures only further segregated them from their peers; they wanted to fit in, not stand out. This applied especially to children under the age of thirteen. After that age, it's especially hard to determine if an avoidance of native cultural activities is tied to a resentment toward the customs or is simply a typical teenage reaction.

BLENDING TRADITIONS AND CUSTOMS

For people who are considering an intercountry adoption, Holt Children's Services of Eugene, Oregon, has compiled the following questions on culture and tradition:

~ Do you want to learn more about the child's culture and heritage?
~ What characteristics do you think Asian, Indian and Latin American people have?
~ Do you expect your child to have these characteristics?
~ How do you feel about getting lots of public attention because of differences in culture?
~ Do you raise your child to have the same identity as you or your other children?
~ Should your child's name reflect his or her national origin?
~ How can you learn to know what it's like being nonwhite and growing up in a white society if you don't know this from your own experience?
~ Do you feel you are doing a good deed for a poor, homeless child, who will be grateful to you when he or she is older?

If your primary orientation is to help the child become assimilated into your culture at the expense of his own, an agency representative believes that transracial adoption probably isn't the best choice. Parents must have an attitude of respect for the country and culture of the child. The agency suggests that prospective adoptive parents envision a cute little baby growing up into a child, a teenager, an adult and a parent. Finally, they suggest parents ask themselves how they might feel if, when their adopted child matures, he or she considers entering an interracial marriage. Would they embrace that concept easily?

For Debra, a mother of two children born in India, it's difficult to weave the customs of her children's birth country into American culture on a daily basis. "My kids are growing up as American kids in an American family and it's unrealistic to expect them to internalize traditional Indian culture on any more than a superficial level. I've set what I feel are realistic goals for teaching Indian culture to my children. Indian tradition is so different from ours that it's hard to build it into our everyday lives."

Another family recognizes the importance of blending traditions by celebrating many of the traditional festivals of their adopted daughter's birth country as well as the holidays that are part of their own family tradition and of the broader American culture.

Here's what Lisa, the mother in that family, says about The Chinese New Year and Autumn Moon festivals:

The Chinese New Year is actually a two-week festival that in some ways is equivalent to Christmas. It comes at a different time every year and is based on the lunar calendar. Houses are decorated with lanterns and Chinese sayings for prosperity and luck. The sayings are written on red paper with black or gold characters and are hung around the doorways. Traditionally, houses are thoroughly cleaned and all debts are paid. On New Year's Day, after enjoying dinner, the children are given red envelopes with lucky money.

The Autumn Moon Festival celebrates the harvest and is a day for thanksgiving. People eat and eat! It occurs in mid-September and you usually have a picnic and eat mooncakes— pastries with a filling of lotus-seed paste and coconut. Anything round like the moon is eaten on this day.

Though most adoptive parents realize the importance of blending traditions, some families explained that they were just too busy to devote a lot of time to rituals. For a couple who adopted four children from India, all abandoned at birth, just getting through the week continues to be a big challenge, although Sally, the mother, said they do make a point of recognizing "airplane," "adoption," and "citizenship" days. "Even when it's a busy weekday, there's always time for a few reminiscences about the day the phone rang and we heard about them, or the day we went to Immigration to make them citizens." Sally's kids know enough about the culture of India to call friendly Indian adults 'uncle' and 'aunty' (as Indian kids would), and to put their hands together and say 'Namaste' when someone says it to them. They also have pictures of some of the major Indian gods and goddesses hung in their rooms and have visited Indian temples in their area. "The Hindu priests usually take great pains to explain things to them so they won't feel left out."

Though they don't celebrate Indian holidays every year, when they do, they make sure to include all the traditional foods, ceremonies and customs. "We have many Indian people in our area, and we attend Indian events several times a year. My husband and I love Indian food and eat it at least twice a week at home." They wear traditional Indian clothing and jewelry when it's appropriate. Their daughter loves wearing her bangles and "tikkas" (stick-on forehead dots) and wears them freely with blue jeans or her Indian clothes. "I have a lot of recorded Indian music and listen to it when I feel like it. I don't make the kids listen, but they can be a part of it if they wish." They watch Indian programs on their cable system and own Indian art and handicrafts. In addition, every summer the family attends two different Indian heritage camps, where they immerse themselves in Indian culture for several days with other families whose children were born in India. All in all, it adds up to a little bit here and a little bit there, enough to begin building a sense of understanding and pride. She hopes to take all her kids to India before they reach adulthood to help them flesh out their identities as Indian Americans. "But in the end," Sally added, "I can only lay the groundwork; the rest will be up to them."

For Rhonda, living with her family in Texas, a Korean tradition has predicted the future for her two children. She explained, "When a child becomes one year old in Korea, it's a time of celebration. Long ago, babies didn't always live that long, due to smallpox and other diseases." Sometimes infants weren't even given a name until their first birthday. Even now, when the happy day arrives there is great rejoicing.

> The little one is dressed in a brightly-colored outfit and is the center of attention. The family provides a feast of fruits, nuts and sweets. Then comes the game of guess the future. With the members of the family around the child, he or she is placed before a table on which various articles are laid, a book, a paintbrush, money, a bow and arrow. Their future is predicted by what they choose. We have a scholar and an artist.

In Peruvian culture many festivals are based on the Roman Catholic calendar. Some of the major events include Carnaval, Peru's Independence Day, All Souls Day, and Puno Day, which features flamboyant costumes and street dancing in the city of Puno. Unfamiliar with any of these celebrations before they left for Peru, Nancy, an adoptive parent, described another ritual performed on New Year's Eve: "You eat ten black grapes, symbolizing bad luck, while underneath a table, then eat ten green grapes, symbols for good luck. After that," she added, "you run around the block with yellow underwear on the outside of your clothing while carrying a suitcase filled with yellow items." This, according to tradition, insures good travel in the year ahead. She has repeated the custom three times in America since returning with her daughter nearly five years ago.

Tony and Donna described the Haitian customs they've become familiar with since adopting in that country. In addition to their two Haitian children, ages three and one, they have three birth children, 15, 13, and 10 and are foster parents to a 12-year-old multiple-handicapped boy. They have come to love the country of Haiti, the people and their struggle. Donna is currently learning Creole. And their children, like Ann's children from India, attend culture camps whenever possible. "We're collecting Haitian recipes and proverbs, and we also keep in touch with an American support group called 'Haiti in Our Hearts.'" The entire family is eagerly learning about festivals and holidays. In Haiti, she said, "There are more holidays and festivals than days in the year!" Next year they plan on celebrating an African Christmas festival called Kwanzaa, a weeklong celebration that begins on the evening of December 26. A tribute to the deep roots and rich culture of the African People, it's based on seven guiding principles pertaining to spiritual, emotional and intellectual growth. The celebration involves lighting a candle each night and discussing the principle for that particular evening. The words are in the East African language of Kiswahili. Tony and Donna concluded that they wholeheartedly welcome the opportunities to acknowledge their families' diversity.

It's so important to integrate our children's heritage into American culture. Ignorance is so often the root of so many problems. I want my kids to see Native American dances, hear Japanese stories, view Brazilian art. We strongly believe that we come from one creator and plan to celebrate our diversity in this world.

CHAPTER 11

Why Don't I Look Like You?

"No man should be pitied because every day of his life he faces a hard, stubborn problem....It is the man who has no problems to solve, no hardships to face, who is to be pitied ....He has nothing in his life which will strengthen and form his character, nothing to call out his latent power and deepen and widen his hold on life."
—Booker T. Washington, From *My Larger Education* by Booker T. Washington, published by Doubleday, Page, & Co., 1911

EVENTUALLY, THE NOVELTY AND EXCITEMENT OF ADDING A NEW MEMBER TO the family begins to fade. Parents are faced with the job of raising their children into responsible adults while attempting to instill in them the strength to handle life's many challenges. It may not be until a child reaches adolescence that biological parents have to deal with some of the most difficult parenting issues. Parents of adopted children have to be ready for two additional questions posed by their children: where did I come from, and, more commonly with families combining ethnicities, why don't I look like you?

Both questions can be sensitive subjects. With racial differences, comments like, "Is that your baby?" can begin as soon as the infant is out in public. In fact, when Charlie and I attended parenting classes to help prepare ourselves for adopting, we were coached on what a positive response to that question could be. Rather than assuming that the person making this inquiry is simply being rude or callous, assume they might be considering a foreign adoption for themselves and seeking helpful information. The suggested reply was, "Why do you want to know?" It's a response that helps parents keep their emotions under control when it would be easy to become defensive, or, at the very least, slightly annoyed. This response also sets a good example for your child as he or she gets older, an encouragement to look past people's words to what is being implied. It also helps them understand the importance of being private about some matters. After a while, intuition will be your guide in these types of situations.

WHEN AND HOW DOES A PARENT TELL A CHILD THAT HE OR SHE IS ADOPTED?

Are children of three too young to understand an explanation of their heritage? Will they be able to comprehend what a parent is trying to tell them? When is it appropriate to introduce a child to the harsher realities of their background? For Mary, living in Ohio, it was her three-year-old daughter who brought the concept of identity to her attention.

When our oldest was about three, she began to point out that she didn't 'match' us. We told her that people get their color from their birth parents, showed her pictures of her birth mother and her older brother, and chatted generally about skin color. She was also interested in the function of brown skin. I think three is a good age to tell them just about everything.

Some parents do tell their children about their origins when they are only three or four years of age, but there are many exceptions. Our social worker felt that the sooner children are told the truth about their heritage, the better off the family relationship will be, though at an early age, moderation may be the key. Giving children too much information when they are too young can be just as counter-productive as not giving them enough. Parents often know best what their child is prepared to handle. If they have some uncertainties, talking with friends who have adopted, looking for suggestions on the internet, searching for support groups, or seeking advice from the experts are all valid ways to find solutions. In other words, do whatever is required to make this issue as stress-free as possible for both you and your children. Telling a child about his or her heritage may be one of the most important things you do as a parent. And, of course, like all communication, it's not only what you say, but how you say it.

One mother from Texas started explaining the concept of adoption to her children in animal terms.

> We talked about a puppy whose mother couldn't take care of him, so another breed of dog "adopted" the puppy and raised it as its own. We also have a book about a baby bird whose mother leaves the nest; the baby is raised by another bird. We also have talked about how babies grow inside their mother's tummies. Having pregnant friends and relatives helped with this example. Once our kids understood the physical aspects of adoption (that they grew inside another lady's tummy), then we could start working on the psychological part of it.

Exactly how to tell a child that he or she is adopted is a decision that ultimately depends upon a person's comfort level and upon the circumstances of the adoption. Much about a child's birth may be unknown, for example. Some adopted children, especially from China, were abandoned. Parents whose children's adoptions are closed may be legally unable to release all the information they would like to share with their child.

For Dorothy, talking with her son, Skip, about his adoption began early on. She advises parents not to be overwhelmed by the task, or to spend too much time worrying excessively about it.

> The one thing that I have always done with Skip is let him know that he is adopted. He's fully aware of 'what's in the tummy of that fat lady,' as he was surrounded by pregnant teachers while in pre-school. When he started telling us about a baby being in Ms. Jones' tummy, I took advantage of the situation and explained that another lady once had him in her tummy. I went

on to explain that when he was born she gave him to mommy and daddy to live with them forever. He knows why she did it, in his childlike way. He understands the concept of not having any money. He also understands that this woman loves him enough to want only the best for him—all the things she could never give him. Some day, he will meet her.

It's absolutely amazing how much they understand, and with each new piece of information, a new question will form in their little minds. Maybe it won't be asked for a long time, but it will be there. When asked, your answer will lead to yet another question. Don't be overwhelmed. Just be patient, and always remember that you are his or her parent. As adoptive parents, we can't spend all of our time worrying about the 'what ifs.'

I must admit, however, that I'm feeling a little uneasy about speaking to our son on the same topic. My fear of being rejected is lurking around like the Big Bad Wolf stalking Little Red Riding Hood. Charlie and I expect to look upon this opportunity when it arrives as one that will probably resurface and take on many forms throughout the course of Michael's life. It should serve as training for our talks to him about the importance of finishing his homework, helping with the chores, building friendships, being reliable and being on time. It could also give us some experience that will come in handy when it comes time to talk about sex, college, and his long-range goals as a young adult.

If we speak frankly and from our hearts, we will have a solid beginning upon which to build. A popular poem sums up my sentiments. Perhaps an expanded version of this will be shared with Michael someday:

> Not flesh of my flesh
> Not bone of my bone
> but still miraculously my own.
>
> Never forget for a single minute;
> you didn't grow under my heart
> but in it.
> —Fleur Conkling Heylinger

Skin Color, Self-Esteem and Development

Often, it's the introduction of a child into preschool or kinder-garten that magnifies the issue of differences in skin color.

This is usually the first time a child is surrounded by children who are of ethnic origins different from his own or those of his parents.

According to one study conducted in 1994, the effects of cross-cul-tural adoption on the emotional development of adopted children varies. A study of 715 families determined that most adoptive families are thriving; most adolescents who were adopted as infants showed no signs that adoption had a negative effect on their identity development, mental health, or well-being. Conducted by the Search Institute, the study included families that adopted infants between 1974 and 1980 through forty-two public and private adoption agencies in four states: Colorado, Illinois, Minnesota and Wisconsin.

Several factors appeared to contribute to the child's mental health and well-being:

~ strong child-parent attachment
~ shared values and perspectives between parent and child
~ use of effective parenting styles
~ positive, affirming approaches to adoption on specific issues
~ successful management by parents of factors like unresolved
   feelings of loss, feeling stigmatized about being adopted, and lack
   of support for adoption from family and friends

Dr. Peter Benson, president of the institute, stated that the study compared transracially adopted youth with same-race adoptions from a number of different perspectives.

We found that transracially adopted adolescents are doing as well as, if not better than, their same-race counterparts. What seems particularly important is the way parents deal with adop-tion in the family. In the families that are thriving, adoption is a fact of life that is accepted and affirmed, but not dwelt upon. Quiet, open communication about adoption seems to be the key.

The researchers note that the study's findings are particularly relevant for teenagers who were adopted as infants. Children who are placed in homes later in life face additional struggles that were not dealt with in this study. "We cannot overstate the power of early placements," Benson noted. "It is likely the key ingredient in the successful attachment of child to parents and vice versa."

That's not to say there aren't many race-related issues that arise with early placements. Annie, who is a mother of two children—a boy who is half Filipino and half Caucasian, and a Korean daughter—revealed that her adopted son, at three-and-a-half, complained about being tan skinned. He'd rather be white like his mother. Annie's daughter, who is Korean, used to love wearing white tights at her brother's age because they made her skin look white. Ultimately, what made a difference in Annie's daughter's attitude was being around other children of various ethnic origins while attending kindergarten. There she became friends with Hispanic and African American children. "Our daughter was elated that there were other brown kids like her," said Annie, "and some even darker. The comments about not wanting to be so tan stopped."

Another Caucasian mother offers her view on how cross-cultural adoptions can forever change a person's life.

> I'm not sure that those of us with multicultural adoptions do belong to the white middle class anymore. By our adoptions, we have left that particular part of our culture behind and cannot go back. I think we've gone on to something much better. But I know, especially after having lived a year outside of Atlanta in a much smaller city in the South, that what I have is better than what I left. Our Indian child opens us to other cultures that would never be open to us otherwise. And I love the enrichment. We are growing and becoming more cosmopolitan, and I prefer it that way.

COLOR DOES COUNT—JUST ASK HER KIDS

It's difficult to imagine a world where skin color doesn't matter. My husband and I were concerned about Michael fitting into his preschool, into his church, into his baseball team, into his summer camp. After all, fitting in with your peers is important to children. For us, like many other parents having adopted a child of another ethnicity, it's a learning experience, to say the least. Life becomes a look at the world through your children's eyes, and sometimes what a person sees is not pretty. One mother who adopted two Eastern Indian children has lived through some troublesome experiences.

It had to happen someday. It was naive to think it wouldn't. Still, the day I stepped outside to retrieve the morning paper and found the word, NIGGER, spray painted on my front doorstep, my first reaction was utter shock. As the parent of two Calcutta-born children, I had always toed the party line, acting as though I understood what it meant raising children of color—especially in as diverse a place as northern New Jersey. Now I understand a little better, and it hurts.

My children are growing up in an area with many people of Asian and Hispanic descent. There are fewer African Americans, and most of the Asian Indians are a very light brown. So, although everyone is largely very politically correct about it, the bottom line is that my children are often the only "brown people" (their label, not mine) in a particular group. And they notice it. In fact, the kids have been "noticing it" in different ways since they were quite small.

Eddie, now eight, was three-and-a-half years old when his sister Suzie entered our lives, also through adoption. He quickly determined that whoever she was, he definitely did not like her. (Fortunately, in time he came to love her.) On the third night, at bedtime, he was quiet for awhile. Then he said, "Mommy, thank you for my sister who's brown like me." That was the first nice thing he ever said about her. Around the same time, he turned to me while coloring one day, and said, "Mommy? Why do they call people black and white? People aren't black," holding up the black crayon. "And they aren't white either! People are...pink! And brown!" He was right. From that moment, the world's people were classified as either pink (Mommy and Daddy) or brown (Eddie and Suzie). Sometimes, we would hold our arms next to each other and exclaim at how different we looked. But...when we turned our hands palm up, they were all the same color! Different...same!

Having read all the relevant literature, I've always given my children only brown dolls to play with. Lest you think this is intolerably hard core, let me add that I encouraged my (Caucasian) friends and relatives to buy whatever dolls they wished to buy. The Little Mermaid resides in a Barbie motor home next to three brown Barbies, a brown Skipper and three brown babies in Skipper's care. We definitely have an equal opportunity Barbie cupboard.

I honestly have to say that although my friends in other states had faced negative racial incidents, I truly did not expect that experience in the summer of 1995, when we found the ugly "n" word written right on our house. I briefly went mad with grief. Then we called the police, took photographs, and looked for ways to take it off. Within hours, one of our neighbors phoned to say how saddened she was to hear what happened and that the whole neighborhood really felt for us. My feelings are like the eight-inch letters on the front steps: faded, but still readable. Try as we have, we can't find any way to completely get rid of them.

Realistically, people who are very different from each other in a visual way will always be noticed more. A young South Indian man I know was brought up in a Swedish town, where, for years, he was the only brown person he knew. He had a happy childhood as class clown and an adolescence as a snazzy dresser. Yet, when he visited New York City for the first time, he remarked that he could have walked up and down the streets forever. Nobody gave him any notice. He just blended in. He was enthralled. I had a similar experience—in reverse—when I went to live in southern India in 1973 as a Rotary International foreign exchange student. After a few weeks, I came to loathe being out in the streets, where every eye in the world was always fixed on me. I didn't mind so much, though, when the children touched my long blond hair and my pale skin to see if it was real. It certainly made for quite an adjustment.

I think it's probably easier for our kids, coming to us as infants and growing up with us, to adjust to the concept of being visually different almost everywhere they go. Still, while I could forget all about it for long stretches of time, it's not so clear they could. When we attended our first Navratri dance, they excitedly exclaimed, "Mommy! You're the only pink person here!" Suzie recently asked me as cool as can be, "Mommy, when I get my next Mommy can I have a brown one?" Naturally, I informed her that, pink as I am, I am her terminal Mommy! Despite my best efforts, Eddie expressed negative feelings about being brown for a couple of years upon entering school. He still occasionally tries to blame his brownness for difficult relationships, and he recently said that his second-grade teacher thinks he's special because, "I'm the only brown one." Could it be true?

In my great-grandmother's generations, there were only two kinds of people. To the day she died, she referred to my children as "Annie's nigger babies" when someone reminded her of them. I had to stop sending her Christmas cards with photos because this epithet inflamed my grandmother, who has long since found pleasure in the little brown faces. Move five generations forward and you hit my children. A few years ago, I became aware that Eddie had learned very fine distinctions between different kinds of brown people. One evening, we were watching an educational program ("Wheel of Fortune") and I pointed out a new contestant who was a brown, straight-haired woman. I remarked that she looked Asian Indian. He threw her a glance, and said, "Nah, Mom, she's not Indian. She's Puerto Rican."

Last year, Eddie was occasionally called "Leroy nigger" on the school bus. Now, this was a bus for special education kids, a hard-to-control bunch at the best of times. He was a first grader. I was in a dilemma, and I chose the "school of hard knocks" approach. I told him that although it was hard now, he should practice his ignoring skills when people said things like that. I couldn't be in his coat pocket all the time, and even if kids got yelled at by their parents, they would probably just whisper it so the bus driver wouldn't hear. After what happened this summer, I really wonder if this was the right approach. At the time, I wasn't sure what else I could or should do. Now, I have a folder of materials presented at a 1995 conference that a friend brought back for me in the nick of time: "Guidelines for Assertive Expression when Dealing with Racist Remarks" and "Responding to Racism."

While better equipped for the next incident, I still wonder why this had to happen to us. It's probably no accident that we were in the middle of the showy and acrimonious O.J. Simpson trial, with the "n" word bandied about on the airwaves on a daily basis. One of the cops who showed up to take the report at our house tried to console me by saying, "Oh, it was probably just some kid." I definitely don't feel better hearing that. Fortunately, life is pretty correct here most of the time. I truly believe that there are correct feelings behind the incorrect behavior most of the time, but there are still some nasty currents of feeling under the surface. In other words, color counts. Just ask my kids.

Virginia, whose brown-skinned daughter was six years old when she became frustrated with her appearance, acknowledges the truth of that observation. "We never tried to talk our daughter out of her feelings. It is easier to be white, and we openly acknowledged that, all the while telling her that we were absolutely thrilled with her being exactly who she was. I think recognizing this 'white privilege' allowed her to get past it, and to see all the wonderful things there are about being brown." Another parent told me that they affectionately call their son cinnamon toast and threaten to nibble on him.

How to Handle Discrimination

Though most of us know what discrimination is, how do we handle it correctly? According to experts, there are three steps to assertive expression when dealing with racist remarks: describe, express, and specify. Describe the other person's behavior to them as objectively as possible while using concrete terms. Then, describe the offensive action, not the motive, and describe the person's behavior in non-blameful language. Next, express your feelings calmly. Use "I feel" followed by a feeling word, such as hurt, angry, upset, uncomfortable.

Then indicate how the other person's behavior or comments have affected you. For example, "My daughter is _____ and the message that all of her people are stupid and lazy hurts her, and I feel that pain also." Then, depending on the circumstances, you may want to specify a request for future behavior, "Please do not tell jokes about any groups of people when I am around."

Questions Parents Should Ask Themselves to Better Deal with Racism and Discrimination

To check from time to time on how they're handling the difficult issues surrounding race, parents might ask themselves the following questions.

~ Have you helped improve your child's self-esteem by having contacts with other cultures?
~ Have you created an atmosphere of awareness and trust, so that your children will tell you if they're made uncomfortable by racist remarks, learning materials or books?
~ Does your child's school use unbiased learning materials that present a multicultural view? If you feel it may not, talk to teachers, the principal and other parents.

There are dozens of antiracism resources available to help deal constructively with the issue. I've included a partial list of these in the appendix.

Jillian, a Caucasian mom of two African American girls ages eleven and nine, speaks about the surprise she encountered when finding out that living in a racially diverse environment doesn't necessarily shield a family from racial incidents.

I was so happy that there was even a tiny bit of racial diversity in our small school, and naively assumed that the kids of color would band together. Instead, they are in small camps, picking on each other. In our district, the two main ethnic minorities,

Native American and Hispanic, have reached the point of recurring fights and some rival gang identification. They are also mean to the new Russian immigrants.

By contrast, the incidents involving my African American children have so far been random, individual, and pretty rare. Even as I type this, my daughter is spending the night with the little girl (white, age eight) who, a few months ago, was calling her a "black bitch." She came over to play yesterday and while I don't think they are going to be soul mates, we're neighbors, and I'm hoping we can get along. Our name-calling incidents, so far, have always come from white kids, and always from kids under a lot of stress. The neighbor girl was being cared for by her Native American step-relatives because her mom had left her behind. When possible, I talk to the kids in private. I always alert their teachers and the playground monitors, because racist talk can become a fad like any other, although much more harmful than most. One of my daughter's play-mates of many years popped out one day with, "My eyes are blue because I'm full of sky. Yours are brown because you're full of shit." I told her that was offensive and why it was offensive. She said, "It's just a saying. Everybody says it." I said, "Not in this house, so you need to make a choice."

INTERNET BULLETIN BOARDS CAN OFFER MUCH-NEEDED ANSWERS

Parents sometimes look for advice from other parents by subscribing to adoption bulletin boards. One parent concerned over rude comments about her African American daughter's skin color asked through an e-mail message, "What can I do?" In his reply, another parent offers this advice on the subject.

It's an age when kids are starting to categorize the world outside their families, and it's a real shock for kids in multiracial families who don't divide the world that way. The good news is that kids that age are still pretty trusting in adult authority and if you or the teacher keep putting out positive messages about diversity, they tend to follow your lead. First graders also like to know the reasons for different colors and characteristics—why dark skin and kinky hair was a good thing to have in Africa. Why flat noses are the best kind in cold climates and so on. I think it's a lost cause to make people colorblind, but not as hard to help them appreciate different characteristics, to learn that their class benefits from having kids of different colors and cultures.

The educational environment is certainly not the only place where racial injustices erupt. Sometimes they can break out within families. When Jane and Doug were asked by family members what type of child they were considering adopting they replied, "Human." For Cheryl, it was her father-in-law who needed a better understanding of the words he was using when referring to his grandchildren. "We had to sit down," she declared, "and discuss over the phone with my father-in-law our concerns over his language. He used a lot of descriptive words, such as 'those darkies'. We read him the riot act, no more, or we cut off all contact! Since then he's a changed man."

I asked Cheryl how the issue of racism affected her family's efforts to integrate her adopted children's cultural heritage into their own. Among her comments, she cited human ignorance as the cause for many of today's racial problems.

We just came back from a cultural festival in Vancouver where our kids saw families of various ethnic blends. We saw white and nonwhite kids dancing to African music, ate Ethiopian and Haitian foods, as well as hot dogs. I feel that it's important to expose our kids to a large variety of peoples and traditions, so that the walls of racism can start to come down.

As I was reading message after message about racial concerns, I learned that perhaps complaints from children about not fitting in were not about race, per se, but were tied to family resemblances, or rather, a lack of them. An example of this was expressed on the internet during an e-mail discussion on adoption: "I have five kids—four Korean, one biological. My biological child, who looks just like me, has mourned for years that she is white and that she doesn't look like her siblings." One couple I corresponded with decided that selecting a child within their own race was top priority, although not for purely selfish reasons. Linda and Mark reflected upon the pressures today's society puts on children living in mixed families.

For Mark and I, it isn't important what ethnic background our child comes from. In fact, we believe that ethnic diversity will enrich our family. We chose not to consider black children, not because we would have problems accepting the child, but because we think that it would be much more difficult for our families and for society in general, to accept that we are white parents of black children. We also think that the pressures to identify with black American culture, in addition to white American culture, would place an excruciating burden on our child. The unfortunate fact is that racism, which is not limited to white society, is a reality. The question of whether or not to adopt a black child would be quite simple if society were actually colorblind.

The racial tension between people of Asian, Indian, Latin American and other cultures has not been nearly so violent and dramatic as that between white and black cultures in this country. Therefore, it's our opinion that families with white parents of non black children are much more readily accepted.

On the other hand, Georgia, with four adopted children—ages 30, 29, 24 and 5—and one biological child, has a different view of cross-cultural adoptions:

My oldest three adopted children are Afro-American, my biological Anglo, and my youngest son is Hispanic-Apache-Anglo. To all of you seeking to adopt children of other ethnic groups than your own: go for it. Yes, there are problems, but they are all surmountable. Yes, there is discrimination and stupidity, but that exists anyway. You are just seeing it for the first time. Put your shoulders to the wheel and enjoy your kids in spite of the ignorance. Your kids will be stronger for having learned about the diversity of humanity through their own experience. That's not something that parents of kids of the same ethnic group can teach. Three of my adopted kids were older (nine, six and four) at the time of their adoptions. It's more like a marriage when they come with a history. But it's doable if you can let them be themselves. Love came first and then the details. The questions is: is your love strong enough to face the different path you have chosen? I have personally grown because I stepped up to the plate.

REFLECTIONS ON BIRTH MOTHER CONTACT

In many instances the key issue around the adoption is the adopted child's longing to know where they came from and what their biological parents looked like; race enters the picture secondarily. Tied into that concept are letters to and from birth parents. For example, the following excerpt from a message posted from Barb demonstrates a concern over differences in contact with her children's birth parents, a concern that prompts her to solicit advice.

We have two girls, ages five and six. Both are biracial (African American-Anglo) and have different birth parents. The adoptions are closed, but we do send letters to both sets of birth parents through the adoption agency. We know that the birth mother of the older girl receives them, but that the other birth parents do not. The agency holds all of the unreceived letters in case the birth parents ever request information. We have also received a few letters from our older girl's birth mother. All of the letters in both directions are screened by the agency so that identifying information does not get through.

At the time of the adoptions—each girl was about one month old— their older daughter's biological parents sent letters to Barb to share with their daughter when she is older. Since then, they have also received a picture of the birth mother. Their younger girl's birth mother sent one letter at birth, but nothing since. Unresolved for now, they're left with two nagging questions: first, how do they explain to the younger girl about the differences in contact between the two sets of birth parents; and secondly, should they tell their younger daughter of her biological father's pessimistic view of society's intolerance of mixed-race families, a determining factor in his decision to turn his daughter over for adoption?

Frances, who has two daughters through adoption, Angela and Shannon, reveals several examples of how her two daughters relate to the idea of having birth mothers. In the process she offers insight into how young minds can interpret the information we, as parents, give them. Included in her upbeat story is a description of one daughter's idea of a party mom.

Our daughter's birth mom sent us a picture of the two of them at the hospital. We put them in the first page of her baby book so that it was always there any time we looked through it. Sometimes our daughter focused on it; sometimes she didn't. But it became familiar and handy when she needed to understand where her color came from (and who she came from). When she shows her book to friends, sometimes she skips that first page, and other times she doesn't.

A funny thing about birth moms and names: our daughter Angela was born on December 25, and is very proud of the fact that she shares a birthday with baby Jesus. When she was wanting information on her birth mom a few years ago, we met with our social worker, who said that Angela's birth parents were named Sandra and Joseph. Well, somehow she remembered the names incorrectly. Last year, I heard her explaining her birthday to a little friend saying, "I'm like Jesus' little sister, because I was born on his birthday and my birth parents were named Mary and Joseph."

One thought about birth moms and adoptive moms: I once overheard our other daughter, Shannon, whose thoughts about birthdays always turn to party plans, announce to a friend, "Guess what? Besides my mom, I have a party mom." Now that would be a handy way to think of it. A regular, everyday mom, and then, another more glamorous one for those special occasions.

---

[1] A complete 128-page report is available through Search Institute, by calling 1-800-888-7828. Search Institute is a non-profit organization dedicated to research and resource development that address the needs and concerns of children, youth, and families.

CHAPTER 12

Ready to Meet the Kids and Wish Upon A Star?

"BEEJAMMIES," A COWGIRL, LIFE WITH POPSICLES, AND MORE

IT'S TIME TO MEET SOME OF THE CHILDREN WE'VE BEEN DISCUSSING, SO HERE they are, as described by their parents.

TOMMY, 3

Tommy's birth mother is of Irish, English and Scottish descent. My husband and I are German, Native American, Irish, English, and Scottish, so Tommy doesn't look much different from us. As a matter of fact, my two biological daughters both have dark blond hair and blue eyes, and Tommy has light brown hair, so people just take it for granted that he is mine by birth. I even have a couple of friends that insist that he looks like my husband. He does act like his father frequently. Daddy can't make a move without Tommy wanting to do exactly what he's doing. I've had to go out and get him a little wheelbarrow, some tiny work gloves and a toy shovel, so he can help daddy clean up the construction debris from our renovations. It's so cute to watch them working together.

Tommy is of about average height for a three year old. I have a terrible time taking him for haircuts because I always get mushy when they cut his curls. He's a walking question mark. There's nothing in the world that's not worthy of his interest. He loves trains, especially Thomas the Tank Engine. He's a creature of habit, and likes things done in certain ways. ("No, daddy! You can't put the blue sippy top on the red cup! You have to use the red one!") He is still very much attached to his pacifier, though he limits it to sleep time and times of extreme stress (like when he gets a boo-boo). He has a best friend named Joey, who lives next door. He can name all of the common colors, but mixes up brown and black. He can count to ten, but only if he feels like it. He loves music. He doesn't like Barney but does like Sesame Street and Mr. Rogers. He loves his daddy more than gummy worms. If Daddy doesn't like a certain food, he won't touch it. Consequently, he loves fish. He and my husband go to the fish store at least twice a month. Tommy's aspiration in life is to be a train engineer. He has a golden retriever whose name is Tommy's Golden Beatrice. He likes to paint and cut with scissors, though he still needs a lot of practice. He loves taking a bath, but really hates having his hair washed. He doesn't like sudden loud noises. He's allergic to milk, cats, pine trees, and has some seasonal allergies. He can turn on the computer, find and access his own computer games, and knows how to work with the VCR better than I do.

He insists on taking a book to bed with him every night, along with his menagerie of stuffed friends, including his stuffed engine, his spotted dog, two Elmos, seven Grovers, three or four pacifiers, his train pillow, two baby pillows, which he refuses to give up, his regular pillow, and various and sundry cars, trains and small items that catch his interest on any given night. Oh, and he has to have his sport bottle of water on his nightstand, though he rarely takes a drink from it.

He's a homebody most of the time, and would rather hang out in his "beejammies" or underwear than get dressed. He's a terrible eater and would live on Oodles of Noodles, apple sauce and green beans if given the opportunity, with a pizza thrown in once in a while for variety. He likes to help fold laundry or dust the furniture. His favorite colors are purple, yellow and blue, in that order. His favorite number is six.

KELSEY, 3, AND PATRICIA, 4

Both girls can't stand sweets or desserts like donuts, pastries or birthday cake. Kelsey loves rice with everything and can't get enough meat. If she had it her way, she would have lunch meat slices, rice and sauce for every meal. Something funny happened when we were in a checkout line at a store. Patricia was standing beside me and I was holding Kelsey and paying for my purchase. An African Canadian woman was behind me, and when I started to leave, the clerk turned to this woman and said, "My, you have such cute little girls," to which the woman replied, "They're not my kids." I just smiled, because I am Caucasian, and my girls are from Jamaica.

EMILY, 7

My daughter is a ball of nonstop energy—especially her nonstop running of the mouth. She even has long conversations in her sleep! She modeled until she was about 3 years old—one TV commercial and lots of print ads. She loves to read Goosebumps, Magic Attic Club and Boxcar Kids. She also loves Barbie, but baby dolls still win out hands down.

When she was three months old, I wrote a story about her adoption and read it to her almost every night. By the time she was three years old she knew it by heart. When she was in the second grade, she took the little booklet I made and read it to her class. I knew nothing about that until a visit to the school about a month later. Her teacher said that she read it with pride, and had the biggest smile on her face. The class thought it was so cool to be adopted.

CLAIRE, 6

She was born in a remote rural area outside of Calcutta, India, and was abandoned when she was one month old at a health clinic in the area. She was found in a cardboard box on a pile of rags, clinging to life, weighing only two pounds. She was nearly dead from malnutrition and dehydration. An elderly sweeper had dripped milk into her mouth with a tiny spoon, lacking any other equipment. The social workers were on a tour of the area when this old lady came running out of the clinic saying, "Come inside! There is a baby here! You must help her!" They weren't sure they could get her back to Calcutta alive, but they did. Claire has some speech and language issues and also attended pre-k special education. She was declassified for kindergarten this year, and we're hopeful that she'll be able to remain in mainstream classes. Claire is still tiny. She's got quite a talent for gymnastics and the body to go with it. She's not strikingly bright, but her smile makes up for it. She's the sunbeam of the family, with the most infectious giggle you've ever heard.

BRIAN, 18 MONTHS

Brian has been both a joy and a challenge. He had suffered a bout of bronchitis just before he came home and quickly came down with pneumonia after his arrival. He will probably have asthma and allergies and he becomes deathly ill whenever he catches a cold. We use a nebulizer to keep his airway open when he's sick. After testing him for everything under the sun, some very kind people on the internet helped me hit the nail on the head—he was suffering from celiac disease, also known as gluten intolerance. Any foods containing wheat, rye, barley or oats are toxic to him. Once we put him on a gluten free diet, he transformed. He now weighs almost sixteen pounds, and has taken eight steps between mom and dad.

MARK, 17, AND MELISSA, 14

Mark and his sister are like night and day. Mark is short in stature, loves all sports—especially basketball—and has a wonderful personality and lots of friends. I remember one instance when Mark was seven; he had gotten into some kind of trouble, so he was sent to his room. Instead of spending his time silently thinking about his mistakes, I caught him dangling his fishing pole out of his second-floor window to a friend below. On its end—a twinkie! I didn't know what to do. All I wanted to do was laugh. His sister, by comparison, is tall and quite shy around others, though usually the leader within her group. We are currently in counseling. She's having a hard time accepting the fact that she's adopted. It's going to take a long time.

MAI LYNN, 18 MONTHS

Our daughter was found by police officers on March 3, 1995, in a train station in Shanghai. She is the most healthy and beautiful child that I have ever seen. She has just about all of her teeth on top, and half on the bottom. When we first got Mai Lynn, she was taking only two bottles a day with cereals in between. We immediately started giving her more bottles and food. She eats just about everything and especially loves vegetables and fruit. She was teething during the time we spent in China, but it did not seem to bother her at all. She is a very happy and open baby. She learned immediately that when she saw the snuggly carrier, this meant we were going out. She coos and laughs and bounces at this prospect.

KATHLEEN, 8, AND ELIZABETH, 4

Kathleen wants to be a cowgirl when she grows up. She's not a dainty ladylike child. Although she is physically beautiful—very tall and slim—she is insecure with her looks and tries to dress as sloppily as possible. She says that tomboys don't wear dresses, curl their hair or wear pretty clothes. Kathleen has been diagnosed as having Attention Deficit Disorder (ADD), and takes a pretty hefty dose of Ritalin to control it. Her schoolwork is improving every month. With her dark moods and lack of initiative, Kathleen is our serious, brooding child.

Elizabeth has an imagination like no other. She doesn't know what she wants to be when she grows up: it changes with each movie, video or cartoon she watches. Elizabeth loves to imitate mother figures. She's currently infatuated with a set of five toy racehorses that her grandmother bought for her. She's set up a jumping course across the kitchen floor. She's our happy-go-lucky, lighthearted child.

Nick, 4

Nick is very conscious of his neat appearance. He likes his shirt tucked into his pants, and I must always button the top button on button-downs. There's nothing he likes more than a good tickle on the feet at bedtime. He does not like to walk barefoot in the grass because as Nick explains it, "I'm afraid the worms will crawl up my body and onto my head." He's very verbal. He enjoys telling make-believe stories. Though he doesn't like to write or color, he does enjoy painting and playing with his trucks and stuffed animals.

Jim, 10 months

Jim is German. He rolled over at one month and at eight months was crawling all over the place. He goes into everything head first. He is the child that puts everything in his mouth. He loves to chase his older brother around the house by crawling after him.

Nathaniel, 2

Nathaniel has jet black hair, olive skin and is 100 percent Hispanic. He did all the motor skills late because he really loves to watch things and take everything in. He loves to figure out how things work first. He loves playing with the computer and can sit there for hours. We have a special keyboard for the computer and he has Dr. Seuss, and Winnie the Pooh computer games. From an early age, he has been able to pick up words quickly.

Margie, 10

Margie was born in an Army hospital. She stayed in the hospital for five days, not because she was sick, but because our lawyer was trying to get the release of custody from the birth father. She was crawling and going down stairs at seven months of age and started walking at eight months. By ten months she started climbing on everything, at eleven months Margie decided that she didn't want us to feed her any more, so she refused to eat anything but finger foods. By eighteen months we could hardly keep up with her.

We moved to Pennsylvania when she was twenty-two months old. During this time we learned to put locks on everything, including our own room. Margie loved to wander around and look for pretty things, or interesting things. One morning we came down into the kitchen and found Margie sitting in front of the refrigerator, with the door open, cracking all the eggs into her lap. Another day, my neighbor who lived across the street called to say that our daughter had just visited them, unbeknownst to us. We got those slot-type locks and installed them at the top of the door. A few mornings later, at 6 A.M., our neighbors called to say that when they came downstairs for their breakfast, Molly was playing in their family room! We went downstairs to see how she had gotten out. She had pulled a chair over to the door, put a book on top of it and stood on all of this to open the lock!

She loves strangers, especially men who have dark hair and glasses. She began attending a preschool at our local YMCA when she was three years old. She had an imaginary friend, a dinosaur, who flew behind our car on the way to school and who waited for her there in the parking lot. Just after her third birthday, she found my sewing scissors and cut off her below-the-shoulders hair, to above her ears, but only on one side.

MOLLY, 5

We adopted our daughter from Peru. Molly goes to preschool. It took her all year to get the nerve to raise her hand and ask a question. She is content to play Barbies all day, and loves to go the park and play with her best friend, Seth. Last week we got our third letter from her birth mom. We jumped up and down with excitement, but joy turned into tears as our son started to cry. "Where's my birth letter?" he asked. These are the situations we have to contend with these days. Molly would live on popcicles, if we let her. She will always stand out in a crowd with her striking long black hair, dark eyes and beautiful cinnamon-colored skin.

Jason, 1

The first week we returned from Guatemala with our son, we all had the flu. His first month here we dealt with his parasites. The second month, he had head lice and shared them with the rest of the family. Two months later he caught chicken pox and gave it to his sister. The next month he tried out an electrical outlet with my car keys and knocked out all the power in our house. Then he required six stitches above his right eye after falling on a toy. He's turned off the furnace and turned down the water heater, only to turn it up the next week. By the end of his first year in the United States, Jason has been baptized, naturalized, circumcised, notarized and certified. And we wouldn't trade him for the world!

In Tribute to Wishing

Exploring the nature of adoptions wouldn't be thorough unless some words were devoted to what parents wanted for their children and their childrens' lives. It was important to me to hear what other adoptive parents wished, in part, because I was curious to see if those wishes differed in any way from the wishes biological parents may have for their children. In some instances, they did. The wishes of other parents were truly universal.

Go ahead. Dream a little. Consider adopting a child. Wishes do come true.

꒛꒜꒝꒞꒟꒠

I wish for our daughter a life filled with the happiness and security that come from having a loving family. I wish her the creativity to dream her dreams and the confidence and perseverance to pursue those dreams to their fruition.

꒛꒜꒝꒞꒟꒠

What we wish for our daughter might best be condensed from our prayers. "Bless my little girl with good health, bless her with good choices, and most importantly, bless her with a love for You."

❧❧❧❧❧❧

My wish is that someday both children will want to search for their birth parents. I would have no problem with that at all. I see us as one big family. It's just a little different from other people's families.

❧❧❧❧❧❧

Happiness, success and to feel good about themselves. We want more for our children than what we have.

❧❧❧❧❧❧

My wish for my children does not differ from the wish I would have had if I had biological children. I wish happiness for my children. Don't we all? My hope is that my children grow up to be independent adults with strong values and morals. Money is overrated and not important to me. I hope that they realize their strengths and use them in life.

❧❧❧❧❧❧

I wish for each of my children to have happiness and a sense of self worth, an appreciation for different opinions and cultures, the enjoyment of extended family and a love of life. The only difference between my kids is that I also wish my two youngest (adopted) to be comfortable with who they are, as well as at peace with their heritage.

❧❧❧❧❧❧

We hope that our children will become mature, loving, compassionate people with good values and their priorities in perspective. We hope they'll achieve their dreams and accept their failures, but not let failures define their lives. We hope they'll want to be our friends when they become adults. We think that all biological parents wish these things for their children.

❧❧❧❧❧❧

My wishes for my adopted son are the same as for all of my children—that they get a good education and find a place in the world where they're happiest, whether it's at home with children or in a career; and that they find partners who will treat them with respect and love them unconditionally, or that they remain happily single. I really want them to be happy and productive and contribute something to the world, no matter how they choose to do it. I have a few extra wishes for my adoptive son. I wish for him always to be comfortable with who he is and how he got here. I wish for him an understanding that his birth mother loves him and that she didn't abandon him, but made a choice based on love. I wish for him to always have easy access to his heritage, and that he never have to search for something that the rest of us take for granted.

I wish that he always feel good about himself, and to know that his dad and I love him equally with his sisters, who are not adopted. As far as we're concerned, our kids are our kids, no matter how they got here. I wish for him to be close to his sisters. I wish for him to be always a part of his birth family and feel free to love them as much as he wants. Mostly, I wish for him to see an end to closed adoption in his lifetime. I want him to feel that adoption is just another way to make a family and not something that should make him feel different or less worthy.

⁊⁊⁊⁊⁊⁊

The most important thing I wish for my child is that she grow up happy with herself and her place in the world. I hope that this happiness will come from doing what she can to make the world a better place, through whatever means she chooses. But in the end, I would rather have her be happy and a couch potato than a social activist who is unhappy or depressed. I would also like her to feel comfortable in the larger African American community, but again, this is secondary. I would like her to have what I have: good health, a supportive community, a loving family, a challenging and interesting career, and enough economic resources that money is not a source of great stress. But I also know that she is her own person who will make her own way in the world. So I wish for her joy and fulfillment on her journey.

⁊⁊⁊⁊⁊⁊

What I want for my sons is what every mom wants for her children: the best. But my biggest goal for them is that they grow up to have a strong faith in God, as that is what has helped my husband and I through the infertility and the adoption process. We always know that no matter where our children came from, or how they got here, that they are the children God has picked for us.

☙ ☙ ☙ ☙ ☙ ☙

I don't think that these wishes for our daughter are any different from what a biological mother wishes for her child: happiness, health, family, good friends and many opportunities. I wish that she will reach for the stars regardless of how close she comes to touching them. I wish for her love, faith and trust. And I suppose, I wish for both of us a relationship that will nurture and support us.

☙ ☙ ☙ ☙ ☙ ☙

What do I wish for our children? I wish for them to be happy, well-adjusted, "normal" kids. I want our two kids to know the difference between right and wrong and to know how to defend their beliefs. I want them to choose their friends wisely. I want them to explore all the opportunities for careers and to make their choices based on their personal interests. I want them to go to college and learn about the world. I want them to respect their elders and listen to what they say.

☙ ☙ ☙ ☙ ☙ ☙

MORE ABOUT MICHAEL

Charlie and I recently celebrated the first anniversary of adopting our son and I have a few confessions to make. During this past year, I have become decidedly addicted to cuteness, sweetness, innocence and awe. Make that cuteness with a capital "C". And the inevitable has happened. I have plunged headfirst into a refound appreciation for an endless number of things, things like the nonchalance of an autumn leaf as it drifts through the air—one end turning up, then down, sometimes completely turning over as it makes its way to earth, blowing to the left a little, then to the right, never an uninterrupted line to the ground. Things like the scratchiness of a pine tree's trunk, and the smoothness of a stone. I've discovered again an appreciation for all things that creep, crawl and fly (not to mention buzz, hiss, howl, chirp, croak, whinney and bark). I've also rediscovered playgrounds with the molded plastic, larger-than-life squirrels, ducks and bears that go bumpity-bump. And I'm appreciating all over again the smell and stickiness of grape, cherry, and orange popcicles, and the different ways you can lick them. All of them things I'd forgotten for so long.

Our son is no longer a little dough ball, easily pliable, most comfortable being on the floor. He's up, and the rest of his world is up even higher. One day I lowered myself to his earlier infant's level to see what it was like and cruised around the house. What I saw: a few cobwebs in the corners, five Cheerios underneath the cocktail table, missed milk stains splattered on furniture legs, the hidden world that's underneath tables, chairs, desks, lamps, and beds, and the goodies it contains— crayons, rubber bands, a headband, a pencil, an overdue library book, even my favorite silver watch that had mysteriously disappeared. I saw a few potential hazards, too: cords, plugs, slick wood floors, weighty books, and tablecloth edges dangling close to the floor.

When Michael was nearly two years old, he liked to "feed" potato chips to his Barney slippers. It made sense to him. The opened mouths of the slippers on his feet seemed to invite the obvious. When the chips remained uneaten, he threw them to the floor with a disgusted, perplexed look upon his face.

In the mornings he often approached our bed and pleadingly, without being able to say the right word, asked me with his big brown eyes to 'Please pull my special blanket up onto your bed, too.'

He liked to roar like a lion and chase me around the house. After one recent session, I ended up with a broken toe. The same toe, ironically, that had been broken once before. He slept with his Sad Bear, Seal Man, and Pooh Bear, with a horse that whinnies, a white musical teddy bear, and a nonmusical pink one whose fur he liked to chew on. Sometimes he liked to stuff the chewed-off bear fur into his ears. He was greatly amused by taking his socks off during nap time and throwing them out of his crib. As I hunted for them day after day, he broke into unrestrained laughter. Recently, we diapered Pooh Bear at my son's nonverbal insistence. The word "yucky" has not only invaded my vocabulary, it has taken it over. When I say the word, our son darts his tongue in and out of his mouth in disgust. He giggles incessantly whenever Charlie and I play "horsy" with him on all fours. It's murder on the back and knees, but it's great for the soul.

Age Two and Still Loveable

Since turning two, he's into more sophisticated things like swimming in our bathtub, just like Daddy does in our pool, and pulling his pants down whenever and wherever the mood strikes him. His verbal skills are growing by leaps and bounds. To him, "Ma-Moo" means movie, and so does "Baa-Boo." He knows that cows go "Moo" and that the rooster says "Da-Doo." Ducks say "Kack" and the word "Outside" is shortened naturally to "Side." Everything else is referred to as, "Me" or "Me see." He's now able to hit the note of C and sustain it for long periods, for apparently no other reason than simply to do it.

He likes to lay flat on his back on our blacktop driveway just to see how it feels, and he has learned what a "boo-boo" is. When Michael sees me wearing a nose strip that helps me breathe at night, initially he looks confused, then he points at the foreign object while repeating, "Boo-boo," "Boo-boo." Then he makes a smacking noise with his lips to kiss it and make it better. He noticed a dent on the side of my car, and again said, "Boo-boo," then kissed the hard metal.

During this time I've developed another addiction, an addiction to Sesame Street videos, especially for one movie in particular: *The Best of Burt and Ernie.* I well up with emotion every time it's played and wonder if I would have made a good actress, since I cry at the drop of a hat.

Recently, we received a generous seven-inch snowfall. It was our first experience with a sled and with eating snow. I was anxious to see if my son would exhibit the same exhilaration as I do for these wonderful seasonal opportunities. Happily, I can report that the sledding went well, and so did the snow eating. He's a natural, though it was up to me to see that he was thoroughly prepared. Were his mittens on? Both of them? Where were his thumbs? Boots secured? Little heels all the way down into the shoe? Snowsuit zipped? Hat tied? Kleenexes in my pocket? Sunscreen on his cheeks? My mind was racing ahead to the preparation that would be necessary when he attends camp for the summer. Once, when the plastic sled gained too much momentum, he rolled off onto the packed white stuff and reminded me of a bowling ball rolling slowly down the lane. When I dusted him off, he was smiling like a true champion. I was proud. Sledding with my two-year-old was like managing a prize fighter. After each round with the hill, instead of wiping him off with a towel, squirting him with water, and giving him a pep talk, I brushed off his clothes, offered him his sippy cup, cheered him for his efforts, then pushed him back down. Happily, I can also say that if this outing was any indication of a permanent appreciation for sledding, I will have succeeded in passing along to our son my most favorite family tradition. Now, all we have to do is work on picking cherries.

I've expected the terrible twos to arrive for some time now. Everyone around me warned of their dreaded and imminent appearance, even strangers like checkout clerks. "How old is he?" they'd inquire, after telling me how absolutely adorable he was. "Almost two," I'd answer. Immediately their kind, smiling faces turned to expressions of deep concern. "Good luck," or, "I see, you have my sympathy," were common replies. Consequently, my thoughts drifted to Ivan the Terrible, Caesar, and Blackbeard. I envisioned the worst.

"Anywhere from 18 to 30 months is typical," said my pediatrician about the age this affliction can develop. "Don't be afraid to leave the situation if it gets out of hand, as much for the parent as for the child. I've left my cart full of groceries in the store, pulled my hat down over my head so none of my patients recognize me, and taken my son kicking and screaming from the store." I asked myself, "If the terrible twos were bad for my pediatrician, what would they be like for me?"

Though my husband and I are not out of the woods just yet, at twenty-five months, we're still waiting for something terrible to happen. Sure, he's had little flare-ups, but no more than his mother and father. "I hope he's not a biter," a friend of mine said. "The kids pick it up at preschool." So far, no marks. And when he does feel the need to scream and release a little frustration, rightly or wrongly, I have instituted a policy: "Michael, it's OK to scream if you want, but please do it in your happy room or in some place other than Mommy's ear." Instead of the worst, our son has given us the best. End of that story.

He's given a richness to our lives that would simply not be possible without him. He's already taught us a lot about ourselves, about traits we never knew we possessed, and in some cases has given us the desire to improve upon some of our less attractive ones—like the lack of patience. Because of our son, when my husband, forty-five, and I, thirty-nine, say "goodnight" to each other, we say, without consciously planning it, "Nighty-night." And when we lay our son down to sleep for the evening, we've formed the habit of telling him that we love him more than the whole wide world with everything in it, just as my mother and father did with me. When it's my turn to tuck him in, I sometimes look up to the framed poem written by an unknown author that's hanging on his bedroom wall:

Once there were two women who never knew each other
One you do not remember, the other you call, Mother.

Two different lives shaped to make your one
One became your guiding star
The other became your sun.

The first one gave you life
And the second, taught you to live in it.

The first gave you a need for love
The second was there to give it.

One gave you a nationality
The other gave you a name.

One gave you a talent
The other gave you aim.

One gave you emotions
The other calmed your fears.

One saw your first sweet smile
The other dried up your tears.

One sought for you a home that she could not provide
The other prayed for a child and her hope was not denied.

And now you ask me through your tears, the age-old question,
unanswered through the years, heredity or environment,
which are you a product of?

Neither my darling, neither.
Just two different kinds of love.

On those nights when it's my turn to tuck him in, I get all misty-
eyed and warm inside.

ཏ༢ཏ༦༢ས

EPILOGUE

The Story Continues...
Four Years Later

FROM A RECENT PHONE CALL TO THE DIRECTOR OF THE AGENCY WHO HELPED place our son, I gained other meaningful insights into the life of a very special person who was touched by adoption. It began with my asking about the health and well-being of our son's biological mother.

"Did she receive the pictures of Michael we sent over the Christmas holidays?" I asked rather nervously.

"Yes," the director replied. "I personally took them down with me to the Hogar in Guatemala. Our Hogar is where she and other birth mothers can come and get information about their children who have been adopted. Michael's mother came in just before Christmas." I immediately began wondering what she looked like, what kind of woman she was. "Were you able to take her picture so that we could share it with Michael?" I asked.

I did ask her. But she said maybe next time she comes into the city. She felt on that particular day that her hair was unkempt, and that she was not dressed properly for it, though she looked very nice to me in her native dress. I began by asking her if her life was good at the moment, to which she replied, 'Yes, I am working in a clothing factory in the mountains.' She had traveled a long way to get to the Hogar that day in anticipation that perhaps some information, a letter, a picture, a little momento might be waiting for her. You would have thought that I had given her the moon when I handed her the pictures of Michael. She looked like a tremendous weight had been suddenly lifted from her shoulders. You should have seen her face—she was beaming. Then she said to me, 'You have given me the greatest gift.' And I said, 'No, it is you who gave the greatest gift.'

Though we had updated her in previous years, she made many of the same inquiries about Michael again. In her native language, Spanish, our son's biological mother asked if her son was still healthy and with a good family. The director reassured her.

Yes, he is. He is with a wonderful family and he is healthy. This I had told her in past visits, but for some reason, this time, my words seemed to carry more meaning. She knelt down and cried. I asked her why she was crying, and she said to me, 'These are not tears of sadness, these are tears of joy.'

By now, tears were streaming down my cheeks and onto the speaker of the telephone receiver. It struck me profoundly that unconditional love never dies. What else in life has such power?

After a long silence, I regained my composure and found my courage. I asked the director if she felt it would be realistic to tell our son that there could be an opportunity for him to meet his biological mother.

Yes, it's quite possible, though I'd recommend waiting until Michael is at least seven or eight years of age. We would have social workers accompany you on the trip. But I want to warn you now, some children have by that age developed a fairy tale story about their biological parents. With some children, meeting their biological mothers and fathers can be traumatic. For other children, it can be quite a positive, uplifting experience.

I found myself appreciating her honesty. Would our son choose to go? Or would he not? Would he be confused? Would he be saddened to see a woman looking older than her years, realizing the hardships of her nomadic life? Or would he be, instead, moved by her? Would he wonder about his biological father and where he lived? Would he come away feeling even prouder of his heritage and more knowledgeable of his country of birth?

As I hung up the phone, visualizing the images created by our conversation, I asked God to bless our son's Guatemalan mother on that day and to fill her with a resonating peacefulness in the decision she made almost five years ago. I routinely continue to pray that every night when she lays her head down to sleep somewhere in the Guatemalan countryside, hundreds of miles from our home, and cultures apart, that she finds comfort in knowing that we are forever connected to her through her giving us, truly, our life's greatest gift, a son.

APPENDIX 1

Ten Tips For a Better International Adoption Trip

1. Get to know the lay of the land before you travel. Buy guide books and click through the hundreds of links in AdoptionTravel.com.

2. Arrive a couple of days before you are scheduled to meet your child so you can acclimate to the time change and the culture. This is especially important if you are a first-time parent and/or this is your first trans-Atlantic or trans-Pacific flight.

3. Bring every over-the-counter medication you think you might need: antihistamine, acetaminophen, melatonin (for jet lag), and a bottle of Pepto bismol.

4. Bring a few of your favorite comfort foods.

5. Bring a copy of your entire dossier—including a photocopy of your child's VISA approval (II71-H).

6. If you are adopting a baby, don't bring a lot of baby food in jars. Wait until you are home to introduce your child to new foods.

7. Consider packing an umbrella stroller. It folds up easily, and is a lighter weight than a carrier type.

8. Save money—fax notes home. Send e-mail if you can find a connection.

9. Before you leave, make an appointment with the pediatrician for a complete medical examination once you return, including stool and blood work.

10. Before you go, prepare your kids at home for the separation and for the new arrival.

INTERNATIONAL REQUIREMENTS

For people considering international adoption, the following list includes basic information on adoption requirements in eight countries as well as a partial listing of agencies with active programs in those countries.

CHINA ⌇
Bethany Christian Services

Children from nine months to 15 years of age are available. Referral wait is two to six months. Parents must be between 25 and 45 years of age and be married for at least two years. Single women are accepted. Parents must travel for one week.

COLUMBIA ⌇
Commonwealth Adoptions International

Parents 36 years and younger can adopt infants. Parents over 36 can adopt older and special needs children. Single women 45 years or younger can adopt. Travel usually occurs 30 days after child commitment. The in-country stay varies from three to eight weeks. Both parents must travel.

ECUADOR ⌇
Villa Hope

Infertility is generally required and applicants must be between 30 and 40 years of age and married at least five years. Parents up to 45 years of age are considered for older children. No single applicants are accepted. Preference is given to childless couples.

GUATEMALA ⌇
Casa Quivira

Many healthy infants are available for immediate referral. Married couples, single women, or single men are eligible. There are no age requirements. After your dossier is complete, the adoption process takes approximately four months. Average travel time is three days. Escorts are available if you do not want to travel.

INDIA 〜
Dillon International

Many children are available in India. Applications are accepted from couples and single women 25 to 45 years of age who have no more than three children. Families usually wait three to five months for a referral of an infant. More boys are available than girls. Children may be escorted to the United States.

ROMANIA 〜
Love Basket

Children as young as nine months are available. Total time to place a child is approximately nine to twelve months. Parents must be believing Christians. Both singles and married couples will be considered. There are no parental age restrictions at this time.

RUSSIA 〜
Cradle of Hope Adoption Center

Children are available from ten months of age and older. The wait for referral is approximately four months after completion of paperwork. Adoptive parents should expect to spend two to three weeks in Russia.

VIETNAM 〜
Children's Hope International

Couples and singles may apply. Vietnam has no age requirements for adoptive parents. Most families can expect a referral within two to four months and can expect to travel two to four months after referral. Approximate length of stay in Vietnam is two to three weeks.

Keep in mind that different agencies dealing with the same country may have different programs and requirements. If you don't fit the criteria of a particular agency, keep asking around, until you find one that fits your needs.

CULTURE CAMPS

General ∿

Holt International Childrens Services sponsors a summer camp for internationally adopted children ages 9 to 15, held in several regions throughout the country. Counselors are primarily adoptees. For more information contact Holt at P. O. Box 2880, Eugene, OR 97402 or visit their web site: info@holtintl.org

Hands Around the World ∿

A summer camp for adopted children and their siblings to enhance self esteem, while embracing many diverse cultures. The camp programs are: African American, Chinese, Eastern European, Eastern Indian, Korean, Latin American, Philippine, and Southeast Asian. Contact Gail Walton for more information at 1417 East Miner Street, Arlington Heights, IL 60004 or email: HANDSATW@aol.com

INDIA ∿
Camp Bharat

Held at Whidbey Island in the Puget Sound area of Washington State. Children need to be over seven years of age to attend. Includes history, culture, food, dance, music and more. Write to the IAWW (Indian Association of Western Washington) at P. O. Box 404, Bellevue, WA 98009 for more information.

KOREA ∿
Kamp Kimchee

Held in Minnesota. Korean culture camp for Korean adoptees and their families. Classes are offered for children from four years old to 12th grade. Visit their web site: KampKimchee.org for more information.

PERU ∿
Peruvian Adoptive Families Convention

Held in Wisconsin. A national gathering of Peruvian adoptive families held during the summer. For more information, call Diane Anderson, 651/439-6749.

The VHP Family Camp

A summer camp designed for the entire family to learn about Hinduism, India and Indian culture. Held in Tolland, Massachusetts. Visit their web site: eden.rutgers.edu/~mittal/vhp.htm for more information.[1]

---

[1] A partial listing of culture camps. For more information, enter key words—adoption culture camp on the worldwide web. Information and listings are constantly being added and updated.

APPENDIX 2

Books, Web Sites and Other Resources on Adoption

GENERAL INFORMATION

〜Adopt America Network
  Web site: www.adoptamerica.org

〜Adopt International
  1/800/969-6665
  Web site: www.adopt-intl.org

〜AdoptioNetwork
  Web site: www/adoption.org/adopt

〜adoptionHELP!
  Site contains information and resources for both adopting a
  child and putting a child up for adoption.
  Web site: www.webcom.com/~nfediac/

〜Adoption Mailing List
  List includes triad members—adoptive parents, birth parents
  and adoptees—from the United States, Canada, Australia, Europe
  and New Zealand, as well as adoption professionals.

To be added to the list, e-mail: adoption-request@think.com
and ask to be added to the list.

⌒Adoption Web Site Book
Contains over 150 adoption web sites.
1/800/894-9518

⌒Adoption TODAY Magazine
246 S. Cleveland Avenue
Loveland, CO 80537
email: louis@lanminds.net
1/888/924-6736
Articles cover a range of interests to members of the triad: adoptive parents, birth parents and adoptees. Also encourages stories from triad members and professionals.

⌒AdoptionSearch.com
Web Site: www.adoptionsearch.com

⌒Adoptive Families of America
Offers publications and has 200 affiliated support groups.
1/800/372-3300
Web site: www.adoptivefam.org

⌒Families Adopting Children Everywhere (FACE)
Publishes a resource guide and magazine.
P. O. Box 28058
Northwood Station
Baltimore, MD 21239
410/488-2656

⌒Foster Parents Home Page
A good source of information for foster parents
and adoptive parents.
Web site: www.worldaccess.com/~clg46/

~National Adoption Center
   Publishes national adoption listings.
   1500 Walnut Street, Suite 701
   Philadelphia, PA 19102
   1/800/862-3678

~National Adoption Information Clearinghouse (NAIC)
   Has free articles on many subjects, including intercountry
   adoption, open adoption, searching for birth relatives,
   school issues, explaining adoption to your child.
   NAIC also has a database of adoption literature on many topics.
   5640 Nicholson Lane, Suite 300
   Rockville, MD 20285
   301/231-6512
   Web site: www.calib.com/naic
   e-mail: naicinfo@erols.com.

~National Council for Adoption
   Gives general information on legislation
   relating to adoption.
   1930 17th Street NW
   Washington, DC 20009
   202/328-1200

~National Federation of Open Adoption Education
   Web site: www.webcom.com/~nfediac/

~North American Council on Adoptable Children
   Organizes support groups.
   970 Raymond Avenue, Suite 106
   St. Paul, MN 55114
   612/644-3036

~SIBSEARCH
   Helps locate siblings of foreign-born children.
   P. O. Box 96
   Bogota, NJ 07603
   201/836-1747

SPECIAL-NEEDS ADOPTION

~Attachment Disorder Parents Network
(ADPN) Newsletter
Contact: Gail Trenberth
P. O. Box 18475
Boulder, CO 80308
303/443-1446

~Attachments Newsletter
Quarterly newsletter with articles by doctors,therapists,
teachers and parents working with attachment
disorder (AD) children.
Write for subscription to:
ACE, P. O. Box 2764
Evergreen, CO 80439

~National Resource Center for Special-Needs Adoption
Offers materials and advice.
16250 Northland Drive, Suite 120
Southfield, MI 48075
810/443-7080

INTERNATIONAL ADOPTION

~Adopted Child
Website:
www.moscow.com/Resources/Adoption/Adoption.html

~Americans for International Aid and Adoption (AIAA)
877 S. Adams Road
Birmingham, MI 48009-7026
810/645-2211

~Buenas Noticias Newsletter
Published by the Latin American Parents Association.
To subscribe, contact:

Bonnie Alvarez
2116 Great Falls Street
Falls Church, VA 22043
or e-mail: BonnieA@aol.com.

~Friends of Children of Various Nations (FCVN)
1756 High Street
Denver, CO 80218

~Guatemalan North American Families Newsletter
For subscription information,
e-mail: GWD@halcyon.com.

~International Concerns Committee for Children
Publishes an international adoption report.
911 Cypress Drive
Boulder, CO 80303
303/494-8333

~Latin American Adoptive Families
Web site: www.gems.com/adoption/laaf/

SINGLE-PARENT ADOPTION

~Single Parent Adoption Network
e-mail: Onemomfor2@aol.com

~Single Parents Adopting Children Everywhere (SPACE)
Offers advice and newsletters.
P. O. Box 15084
Chevy Chase, MD 20825
202/966-6367

ANTIRACISM CONTACTS

~Children's Book Press
Multicultural literature and audio cassettes for children.
1461 Ninth Avenue
San Francisco, CA 94122
510/655-3395

~Children's Literature Association (CLA)
A nonprofit organization devoted to promoting serious
scholarship and criticism in children's literature.
Special Interest Groups:
Minority Literature, International Children's Literature.
P. O. Box 138
Battle Creek, MI 49016
616/965-8180

~Multicultural Review
Dedicated to a better understanding of ethnic, racial and
religious diversity.
10 Bay Street
Westport, CT 06880
203/226-3571

~National Association for the Education of Young Children
Works to improve the quality of services to children from
birth to age eight. Offers books, brochures, videos, posters.
509 16th Street N.W.
Washington, DC 20036-1426
202/232-8777

SUGGESTED READING

Burlingham-Brown, Barbara, *Why Didn't She Keep Me?*, Merle Distributors, 1994.

D'Antonio, Nancy, *Our Baby from China: An Adoption Story*, Albert Whitmand & Company, 1997.

Fahlberg, Vera, *A Child's Journey Through Placement*, British Agencies for Adoption and Fostering, 1991.

Foge, Leslie and Mosconi, Gail, *The Third Choice,* Creative Arts Book Company, 1999.

Gritter, James, *Adoption Without Fear*, Corona Publishing, Co. 1989.

Hopkins, Mary, *Toddler Adoption: The Weaver's Craft*, Perspective Press, 1997.

Karen, Robert, *Becoming Attached*, Oxford University Press, 1994.

Kearney, Brian, *High-Tech Conception*, Bantam Books, 1998.

Melina, Lois, *Raising Adopted Children*, Harpercollins Trade, revised edition 1998.

MISCELLANEOUS

~Tapestry Adoption Book Catalog
An excellent source for adoption books.
To request a free copy of their catalog, call
1/800/765-2367.

Signature Photography

BETSY BUCKLEY was born and raised in a suburb of St. Louis. At age thirty-six, she fulfilled her dream of becoming a parent by adopting her son Michael from Guatemala. Filled with excitement, unanswered questions, and a desire to learn about other adoptive experiences, she began her research for The Greatest Gift. She lives with her husband, son, and daughter, Christie, who was also adopted from Guatemala. She continues to write and is involved with International Families in St. Louis, a multicultural support group for adoptive families.